PAT BROWN, MBA

# HockeyMoney101

*Using Hockey to Teach the Basics of Money*



ABRAM • 47 • BROWN

*First published by AbramBrown47 2026*



*First edition*

*ISBN: 978-1-967737-54-3*

*This book was professionally typeset on Reedsy.*
*Find out more at reedsy.com*

# Contents

# Foreword

Hockey teaches you early that nothing happens by accident.

Every shift matters. Every rep in practice shows up in the third period. Every decision, whether it looks important in the moment or not, adds up over a long season. The game rewards preparation, discipline, and players who understand their role within the system. It punishes shortcuts, ego, and impatience.

Money works the same way.

Most athletes do not struggle financially because they lack intelligence, work ethic, or competitive drive. They struggle because no one ever taught them how the game off the ice actually works. The rules are different. The feedback is delayed. The consequences often do not show up until years later, long after the decision was made.

In hockey, you would never step onto the ice without understanding positioning, line changes, defensive responsibilities, and situational awareness. Yet many athletes enter adulthood and financial independence with none of that structure. They are expected to manage income, taxes, investing, credit, insurance, and long-term planning without a playbook. When mistakes happen, people call it irresponsibility. In reality, it is a lack of coaching.

That is why this book exists.

Hockey Money 101 is not about turning you into a financial expert. It is about giving you a system. A framework. A way to think about money that matches how you already think about the game. Shifts instead of shortcuts. Seasons instead of highlights. Structure instead of chaos.

The best hockey players are not the ones chasing big hits or low-percentage shots every shift. They are the ones who manage the puck, change lines on time, stay positionally sound, and trust that consistent execution will win over time. Financial success follows that same pattern. You do not need to win every shift. You need to avoid blowing assignments that cost the game later.

This book is written for players who understand sacrifice, delayed gratification, and accountability. For athletes who have been coached hard and respect systems that work. For those who know that championships are built in practice, not on the scoreboard.

You will not find hype here. You will not find promises of quick wins or guaranteed outcomes. What you will find is a clear translation of financial fundamentals into hockey language. Budgeting becomes puck management. Investing becomes line construction. Risk management becomes defensive responsibility. Rebalancing becomes mid-season adjustments. Mental discipline becomes staying composed when momentum shifts.

Hockey players already understand long timelines. You train all offseason for a season that might not go your way. You show up anyway. You trust the work. Financial independence is no different. It is built quietly, shift after shift, decision after decision, long before anyone notices.

Whether you played youth hockey, junior, college, pro, or just competed seriously for years, the lessons still apply. The uniform may come off, but the mindset does not have to. The discipline that made you successful on the ice can protect you and your family for decades if it is pointed in the right direction.

This book will not replace professional advice. It will not make decisions for you. What it will do is give you clarity. It will help you understand what matters, what does not, and how to stop beating yourself with unforced errors off the ice.

The season is long. Careers change. Life throws bad bounces. That is unavoidable. What is avoidable is entering those moments without a plan.

Hockey Money 101 is your playbook for the long season ahead. Not to win every shift, but to stay in the game, protect what you earn, and finish strong.

# Introduction

Hockey players understand something that most people outside the game never fully grasp.

A season is not won in October. It is not lost after one bad weekend. It unfolds slowly, shift by shift, game by game, through injuries, slumps, hot streaks, and momentum swings. The teams that survive are not the ones chasing early headlines. They are the ones built to last.

Your financial life works the same way.

Most money problems come from thinking too short term. One contract. One paycheck. One investment. One big decision. Athletes are often surrounded by urgency. Perform now. Produce now. Capitalize now. That mindset works on the ice. Off the ice, it can quietly sabotage long-term stability.

This book starts with a simple truth. Financial success is not about winning one shift. It is about surviving and thriving over a long season.

In hockey, you would never expect a player to stay on the ice for sixty minutes straight. Shifts exist for a reason. You manage energy. You rotate lines. You trust the system to keep everyone effective deep into the third period. Financial life demands the same approach. You pace spending. You manage risk. You make decisions that keep you fresh for later stages of life, not just the early ones.

Many athletes struggle financially not because they lack discipline, but because the timeline changes after sports. In the locker room, feedback is immediate. Miss an assignment and it shows up on film the next day. Blow coverage and it costs a goal right now. Money does not work like that. The feedback is delayed. A bad financial decision today may not hurt for years. By the time it does, the moment that caused it is long forgotten.

That delay creates false confidence.

A player might feel fine skipping defensive responsibilities for a shift or two. It does not always cost a goal immediately. Over time, it catches up. Money works the same way. Overspending. Ignoring savings. Chasing risky opportunities. None of it feels dangerous in the moment. The damage compounds quietly.

Hockey players also understand attrition.

Bodies break down. Roles change. Ice time fluctuates. A player who was on the top line at twenty-two may be fighting for minutes at thirty. Financial life mirrors this reality. Income changes. Careers pivot. Health becomes a variable. Responsibilities increase. A plan that works early must evolve or it will fail later.

This is why the idea of a "set it and forget it" financial plan rarely works for athletes. The season changes. The league adjusts. Your financial strategy has to do the same.

Another lesson hockey teaches is that effort alone is not enough.

You can skate hard every shift and still be out of position. You can win battles and still lose the game. Structure matters. Systems matter. Knowing when to dump the puck and when to carry it in matters. Financially, working hard and earning money is important. Without structure, that effort leaks out through bad decisions, poor planning, and avoidable mistakes.

This book is not about perfection.

No team plays a perfect season. No player has a mistake-free career. The goal is not to eliminate errors entirely. The goal is to reduce unforced errors and stay competitive over time. That mindset changes everything.

Instead of asking, "How can I make the most money right now?" the better question becomes, "How do I stay financially strong for decades?"

Instead of chasing the biggest return, you focus on durability. Instead of reacting emotionally to every market move, you stay disciplined. Instead of letting one decision define you, you stack smart shifts.

Hockey players also know the value of preparation without guarantees.

You train all summer with no promise of ice time. You lift knowing injuries can still happen. You study systems that may change. You prepare anyway.

Financial planning is no different. You cannot control markets, economies, or timing. You can control habits, structure, and decision-making.

This book will ask you to think like a veteran player, even if you are early in your career.

Protect the puck.

Change lines.

Trust the system.

Play the long game.

Financial independence is not about domination. It is about sustainability. It is about keeping options open. It is about finishing strong, not burning out early.

The season is long. Your financial life is even longer. This book is about learning how to manage both, one smart shift at a time.

# About This Book

Hockey is a sport built on details that most people never see.

From the outside, it looks fast and chaotic. Inside the game, it is structured, disciplined, and deeply strategic. Shifts are timed. Lines are matched. Systems are drilled. Everyone has a role. The best teams are not the flashiest. They are the ones that make fewer mistakes, protect the puck, and stay composed when the game turns against them.

Money works the same way.

To someone without a framework, finances feel overwhelming. Accounts, taxes, investments, insurance, debt. It looks like a blur of decisions moving too fast to control. For athletes, this feeling is amplified. Money often shows up suddenly, without preparation, education, or a clear system to manage it.

This book exists to slow the game down.

Hockey players already understand concepts that matter far more than raw talent. Positioning beats speed. Anticipation beats reaction. Discipline beats effort when effort is undirected. You do not win games by skating harder every shift. You win by playing within a system that works over time.

That same mindset is the foundation of sound financial decisions.

Throughout this book, hockey is used as the primary language for understanding money. Not as a gimmick, but as a translation tool. If you understand forechecks, line changes, defensive zone coverage, and momentum swings, you already understand more about money than you realize. You just have not been shown how to connect the dots.

For example, budgeting is not restriction. It is puck possession. When you control where the puck goes, you control the pace of the game. When you lose possession, you spend the shift chasing. Investing is not gambling. It is system-based offense. You set plays, move the puck, and accept that not every shot goes in. Insurance is not pessimism. It is goaltending. You hope it never has to steal a game, but when it is missing, nothing else matters.

Hockey also teaches patience in a way few sports do.

A single shift rarely decides a game. A single game rarely decides a season. Success comes from stacking small advantages. Winning board battles. Making clean exits. Avoiding turnovers. Over time, those details tilt outcomes. Financial progress works exactly the same way. Small, consistent decisions outperform big, emotional ones.

This book is written specifically for athletes because athletes are trained differently.

You know how to prepare without guarantees. You understand delayed gratification. You have lived inside systems where effort is expected, accountability is real, and results are earned. Those traits are powerful in finance when applied correctly. Unfortunately, many athletes are never taught how to apply them off the ice.

Instead, they are handed money without a game plan.

That gap is what this book addresses.

Each section of Hockey Money 101 mirrors the structure of a season. You start with fundamentals. You build conditioning. You install systems. You make adjustments as the year unfolds. You prepare for life after the rink. The goal is not to turn you into a financial expert. The goal is to give you a reliable playbook that keeps you competitive long after the final buzzer.

This book avoids complexity for complexity's sake.

Just like hockey systems, financial systems work best when they are simple, repeatable, and understood by everyone involved. You do not need exotic strategies to succeed. You need clarity, discipline, and consistency. You need to know when to press and when to dump the puck out safely.

You will also notice that this book does not promise shortcuts.

There are no guaranteed wins in hockey, and there are no guaranteed outcomes in money. Anyone telling you otherwise is selling something. What does exist is a process that reduces mistakes, protects you from avoidable losses, and positions you to take advantage of opportunities when they come.

Ultimately, this book is about respect for the long season.

Careers end. Bodies change. Markets move. Life evolves. Players who thrive are the ones who adapt without panic, trust their preparation, and stay committed to fundamentals even when emotions run high.

Hockey teaches you how to do that.

This book simply shows you how to apply those same lessons to money, one shift at a time.

# Foolish Assumptions

Every coach makes assumptions before the season starts.

Not about talent. About mindset.

They assume you want to compete. They assume you are willing to work. They assume you understand that nothing is guaranteed and that results are earned over time. Without those assumptions, no system works. No matter how good the playbook looks on paper.

This book makes a few assumptions too. They are not insults. They are starting points.

First, this book assumes you are competitive.

You may no longer be playing organized hockey. The rink may be behind you. But the competitive drive did not disappear when the skates came off. You still care about winning. You still want progress. You still want control over outcomes instead of reacting to them.

That matters, because financial success requires the same internal edge hockey demands. Not hype. Not aggression. Quiet competitiveness. The willingness to show up consistently, even when no one is watching and no scoreboard is flashing results.

Second, this book assumes you understand discipline better than most people.

You know what it means to do things you do not feel like doing. Early mornings. Repetitive drills. Conditioning work that never makes highlight reels. You already understand that discipline is not about motivation. It is about standards.

That gives you an advantage with money.

Saving, investing, planning, and protecting yourself financially are not exciting. They look boring from the outside. But so does good defensive hockey. The people who skip the fundamentals are the ones who get exposed late in games.

Third, this book assumes you respect systems.

Hockey players understand that individual effort without structure breaks down fast. You cannot freelance on defense. You cannot ignore line changes. You cannot play hero hockey every shift and expect to win over a season.

Money works the same way.

This book assumes you are willing to operate inside a system. Budgeting. Automated saving. Long-term investing. Risk management. These are not restrictions. They are systems designed to reduce mistakes and keep you competitive across decades, not just good months.

Fourth, this book assumes you have made mistakes and will make more.

Every player has turned the puck over at a bad time. Every player has blown an assignment. Every player has taken a penalty they would like back. Mistakes are part of development.

Financial mistakes work the same way.

This book does not assume you are perfect. It assumes you are coachable. It assumes you are willing to learn from errors instead of hiding from them or pretending they did not happen. The goal is not a clean stat sheet. The goal is fewer unforced errors over time.

Fifth, this book assumes you do not want shortcuts.

If you played hockey long enough, you learned to spot shortcuts immediately. The player who skips conditioning. The one who cherry-picks instead of backchecking. It always catches up.

Money has the same traps.

This book assumes you are not looking for a guaranteed win, a secret investment, or a shortcut to wealth. Those do not exist. What does exist is a repeatable process that protects you from bad decisions and positions you to benefit from good ones.

Sixth, this book assumes you are more than just a former player.

Hockey shaped you, but it does not define the rest of your life. Leadership, resilience, accountability, and teamwork travel beyond the rink. This book assumes you want to build something meaningful with those traits, not just look backward.

You are not being asked to relive your playing days. You are being asked to translate them.

Finally, this book assumes you want control.

Not control over markets. Not control over outcomes. Control over behavior, preparation, and decision-making. Hockey teaches you that you cannot control the bounce of the puck, but you can control your positioning when it happens.

Money is no different.

You cannot control markets, taxes, or timing perfectly. You can control your systems, your discipline, and your response under pressure.

If these assumptions feel fair, this book will resonate.

If they feel uncomfortable, that is often a sign you are exactly where this book is meant to meet you.

The goal here is not to impress you. It is to equip you.

No fluff. No hype. Just a clear, disciplined playbook for winning with money the same way you learned to win in hockey: one shift at a time.

# How This Playbook Is Organized

Hockey players do not get handed a playbook and told to figure it out on their own.

The system is installed in phases. First, fundamentals. Then structure. Then situational awareness. Finally, adjustments based on experience, role, and game flow. You learn what matters first, then build on it over time.

This book is organized the same way.

Hockey Money 101 is not meant to be skimmed for tricks or read out of order looking for shortcuts. It is a progression. Each section builds on the one before it, just like a season builds from training camp to playoffs. If you skip steps, things feel confusing. If you trust the structure, clarity improves.

Here is how to use this playbook.

**Front Matter: Setting the Mindset**

The opening sections exist to frame how you should think about money before any tactics are introduced. Just like a coach sets expectations before the first practice, this part establishes perspective.

Money is a long season, not a highlight reel.

Discipline matters more than excitement.

Systems beat talent when talent gets sloppy.

If you rush past this mindset, everything that follows feels harder. This section is about alignment before execution.

**Part I: Fundamentals and Conditioning (Training Camp)**

This is the foundation.

Before teams worry about systems or matchups, they get in shape and clean up basics. In financial terms, this means understanding cash flow, budgeting, banking, credit, and debt.

This section answers questions like:

Where is my money actually going?
Why does it feel tight even when income improves?
Why do small decisions keep compounding into bigger problems?
Nothing in this part is flashy. That is intentional. Just like conditioning work, these chapters prevent breakdowns later. Most financial stress comes from weak fundamentals, not complex investments.
If this section feels uncomfortable, that is usually a sign it is necessary.
**Part II: Defense, Goaltending, and Protection**
Offense does not matter if you cannot protect the net.
This section focuses on risk, insurance, and protection. These chapters exist to keep one bad bounce from wrecking everything you are building.
Here you learn how to:
Understand risk instead of fearing it
Protect income and lifestyle
Avoid catastrophic mistakes that derail progress
In hockey, good defense is quiet. You only notice it when it is missing. The same is true financially. This section is about staying upright through injuries, accidents, and life events that are impossible to predict.
**Part III: Creating Offense (Investing Fundamentals)**
Only after fundamentals and protection are in place does the book shift to investing.
This is intentional.
Investing is not gambling. It is structured offense. Puck movement. Shot selection. Patience. This section explains how markets work, how ownership creates growth, and why discipline beats chasing hot streaks.
You will learn:
What stocks and bonds actually represent
Why volatility is normal
How compounding works over long timelines
Why boring strategies outperform exciting ones
This part is about building offense that can score consistently, not just occasionally.
**Part IV: Managing the Game and the Season**

Good teams adjust.

This section focuses on asset allocation, buying and holding, rebalancing, and managing emotions as conditions change. It connects investing to real life, where careers evolve, families grow, and priorities shift.

Here the emphasis is on:

Line combinations

Mid-season adjustments

Avoiding overreaction

Staying disciplined when momentum changes

This is where many investors fail, not because they lack knowledge, but because they panic or tinker too much.

**Part V: Life After the Rink**

Hockey does not last forever. Financial decisions do.

This section zooms out and addresses taxes, retirement, housing, career decisions, estate planning, and family conversations. These chapters recognize that money is not just about you. It affects people you care about.

The focus here is long-term stability, flexibility, and peace of mind.

**Part VI: Playing the Long Game**

The final section pulls everything together.

It covers advisors, scams, common mistakes, and timeless rules for success. This is the veteran perspective. The reminder that winning is rarely about one move and almost always about avoiding repeated mistakes.

**How to Read This Book**

Read it like a season, not a drill.

Do not rush.

Do not skip fundamentals.

Revisit sections as life changes.

This playbook is designed to grow with you. Just like hockey, the game stays the same, but your role evolves.

If you commit to the structure, the results will follow.

One shift at a time.

# About Pat Brown

Pat Brown understands locker rooms, long seasons, and the quiet discipline required to show up every day prepared. He played college football at the University of Kansas from 1994 to 1999 and was named team captain for the 1999 season. Those years shaped how he thinks about accountability, preparation, leadership, and doing your job even when no one is watching. The lessons learned in the locker room did not end when football did. They became the foundation for everything that followed.

After his playing career, Pat transitioned into financial services and built a career as a financial advisor and wealth manager. He works with individuals, families, business owners, and athletes navigating increasingly complex financial lives. His approach mirrors how teams prepare for a long season. Focus on fundamentals, build systems that hold up under pressure, and avoid emotional decisions that create unnecessary risk.

Pat pursued advanced education alongside real-world experience, earning an MBA and professional designations including ChFC®, RICP®, and CAP®. His work spans financial planning, retirement income strategies, tax planning, and philanthropy. He does not believe financial success comes from tricks or timing. Like hockey, it comes from consistency, structure, and avoiding mistakes that compound over time.

As the college sports landscape changed with the introduction of Name, Image, and Likeness opportunities, Pat saw a familiar problem emerging. Student athletes were gaining access to income, contracts, and endorsements without the education needed to manage taxes, cash flow, business structures, or long-term consequences. Many were learning money lessons the hard way, often after damage had already been done. That gap became the catalyst for his work in the NIL space.

Pat has since become a recognized voice in athlete financial education and has been interviewed by national publications and platforms including Financial Planning, Yahoo, and ESPN Andscape. In those conversations, he consistently highlights the same issue. Athletes are highly trained to compete but rarely trained to manage money once opportunity arrives.

Those experiences led Pat to author a series of practical, athlete-focused books designed to meet athletes and families where they are. His NIL-related titles include Financial Literacy for NIL, Financial Literacy for NIL for Parents of Student Athletes, Financial Literacy for NIL for High School Students, and Financial Literacy for NIL for International Student Athletes. Each book is written to be clear, accessible, and grounded in real-world scenarios rather than theory. The goal is not to overwhelm readers with complexity, but to give them a playbook that actually works.

Pat also created a growing collection of sport-specific financial education titles, including Football Money 101, Baseball Money 101, Basketball Money 101, Cheer Money 101, Dance Money 101, Gymnastics Money 101, Hockey Money 101, Lacrosse Money 101, Rowing Money 101, Soccer Money 101, Softball Money 101, Tennis Money 101, Track Money 101, Volleyball Money 101, and Wrestling Money 101. Each book translates the culture, discipline, and mindset of a specific sport into financial lessons athletes can apply long after competition ends. Hockey Money 101 was written with the same belief. The habits that make great players also make strong financial decisions.

To extend this mission beyond books, Pat founded Former Student Athlete, a platform created to support athletes navigating life after sports. Former Student Athlete provides education, community, and real-world resources focused on financial literacy, career transitions, health, identity, and long-term success once the uniform comes off. You can explore this work at formerstudentathlete.com, financialliteracyfornil.com, and financialliteracy forstudentathletes.com.

Pat is easy to find through a Google search, on LinkedIn, or on Twitter, where he regularly shares insights on athletes, money, and life after sports. His work is rooted in a simple belief shaped by both football and finance. Athletes deserve a better playbook for life after sports, and financial education should arrive before opportunity turns into regret.

Hockey teaches patience, toughness, and respect for the grind. This book applies those same principles to money. One shift at a time.

# Part I: Fundamentals and Conditioning (Training Camp)

You cannot play four lines without a strong foundation.

Every hockey season starts the same way. Training camp. Long days. Early mornings. Conditioning skates that test your lungs and your patience. Drills that feel repetitive. Coaches stressing details that seem basic. Passing. Skating. Positioning. Effort. At that point in the year, no one is talking about playoffs. Everyone is focused on getting their legs under them and building a base that can survive the grind ahead.

That is exactly what Part I of this book is about.

In hockey, you cannot roll four lines if the foundation is weak. If players are out of shape, sloppy with the puck, or unclear on assignments, everything breaks down. It does not matter how talented the top line is. The cracks show over time. Late in games. Late in the season. Under pressure.

Money works the same way.

Most financial mistakes are not caused by complex investing decisions. They are caused by weak fundamentals. No awareness of cash flow. No plan for expenses. No emergency cushion. Poor habits around credit. Banking systems that are disorganized or reactive. These are conditioning problems, not talent problems.

Athletes understand this instinctively. You cannot shortcut conditioning. You cannot fake stamina. You cannot hide poor habits when the season stretches on. Financial life is also a long season. If the basics are not solid, every unexpected expense feels like a breakaway against you. Every opportunity feels rushed. Every setback creates panic.

This section is your financial training camp.

It is where you learn to read the scoreboard. To understand what is actually coming in and going out. To separate needs from wants. To recognize how small, repeated decisions shape long term outcomes. Just like skating mechanics or puck control, these skills are not flashy. They do not get highlights. But they determine whether you are still strong in the third period of life.

## *Reading the Financial Scoreboard*

Before a team can improve, it has to know the score. Coaches obsess over numbers that never show up on highlight reels. Time on ice. Faceoff percentages. Turnovers. Shot attempts. Details that tell the truth.

Financial awareness works the same way.

You need to know:

- What comes in every month
- What goes out every month
- Where leaks happen
- Which expenses are fixed and which are flexible

Most people operate off guesswork. That is like playing a game without looking at the scoreboard. You might feel like you are doing fine. The numbers often tell a different story.

Awareness is not about judgment. It is about clarity. When you see the full picture, decisions stop feeling emotional and start feeling strategic.

## *Separating Needs From Wants*

Training camp forces priorities. You may want to coast. You may want to skip a drill. You do not, because the goal matters more than the moment.

Money requires the same discipline.

Needs keep life stable. Housing. Food. Transportation. Insurance. Core bills. Wants improve lifestyle, but they are flexible. The problem is not wanting more. The problem is when wants crowd out needs or future goals.

Athletes are used to sacrificing in season for a larger outcome. Financial discipline is the same skill in a different arena.

### *Building an Emergency Cushion*

Every team prepares for injuries. They carry depth for a reason. No one plans to get hurt. Everyone knows it happens.

Financially, an emergency fund is your depth chart. It protects you when life throws an unexpected hit. Medical bills. Car repairs. Job changes. Without a cushion, every surprise becomes a crisis. With one, it becomes a challenge you can handle.

This is not fear based planning. It is realism. It allows you to stay calm under pressure instead of making desperate decisions.

### *Credit, Banking, and Organization*

Sloppy puck management leads to turnovers. Disorganized finances lead to stress.

Strong fundamentals include:

- Accounts that are easy to track
- Bills paid on time
- Credit used carefully and intentionally
- Systems that reduce mental clutter

Banking should feel boring and organized, not chaotic. Credit should be a tool, not a lifeline. When systems are clean, mental energy is freed up for bigger decisions.

## *Repetition Builds Strength*

Training camp is repetitive for a reason. Repetition builds muscle memory. Fundamentals become automatic.

Financial habits work the same way.

Saving consistently matters more than saving perfectly. Tracking spending regularly matters more than doing it once. Small habits, repeated over years, create outcomes that look dramatic from the outside.

No single workout makes you fit. No single paycheck makes you wealthy. Consistency does.

## *Money Myths From the Locker Room*

Many athletes struggle here because financial fundamentals are rarely taught. In locker rooms, money myths get passed down like bad advice on tape jobs.

Spend now, figure it out later.

If you make more, the problems disappear.

Debt is normal.

Everyone lives stretched.

Those ideas sound common, but they are the financial equivalent of skipping conditioning and hoping talent carries you.

It does not.

Higher income without structure usually means higher stress, not freedom.

## *Systems Reduce Stress*

When your financial life has structure, stress drops. Decisions get clearer. You stop reacting and start directing.

Budgeting is not about restriction. It is about control.

Saving is not about fear. It is about protection.

Banking is not about complexity. It is about organization.

Credit is not about leverage. It is about responsibility.

Structure removes daily decision fatigue. Just like a system on the ice, it allows you to play fast because you are not thinking about basics.

### *Conditioning Is Invisible Until It Is Missing*

Hockey players know that the teams who last are not the ones that sprint early. They are the ones that manage energy, trust structure, and stay disciplined. Conditioning is invisible until legs are gone in the third period.

The same is true financially.

No one sees your emergency fund.

No one applauds your organized banking.

No one highlights your consistent saving.

But when trouble hits, those fundamentals are the difference between stability and panic.

### *Stabilize Before You Accelerate*

This part of the book is not meant to overwhelm you. It is meant to stabilize you.

When your foundation is strong:

- Investing becomes clearer
- Risk becomes manageable
- Opportunities can be evaluated calmly
- Setbacks become challenges instead of crises

Training camp is uncomfortable by design. It exposes weakness so it can be fixed early. That is what these chapters will do. They help you confront where money feels confusing and replace guesswork with structure. They give you repeatable habits that carry you through busy seasons, tough stretches, and unexpected hits.

You cannot play four lines without conditioning.

You cannot build wealth without fundamentals.

Everything that comes later depends on what you build here.

# Chapter 1: Why Money Feels Confusing After the Final Buzzer

The final buzzer sounds, the handshakes happen, and eventually the rink goes quiet. For most players, that moment does not just mark the end of a game or a season. It marks the beginning of a different kind of uncertainty. During your playing career, life was loud, structured, and constantly reinforced. Practice schedules were posted. Lifts were mandatory. Coaches watched every rep. Film broke down every mistake. You always knew where to be and what mattered next.

Then it stops.

Suddenly, no one is setting your calendar. No one is reviewing your decisions. And for many players, money enters the picture with very little guidance. Paychecks arrive. Bills show up. Decisions pile up. And it feels confusing in a way that surprises people who spent years mastering a difficult sport.

That confusion is not a personal failure. It is structural.

## *Why Financial Literacy Is Rarely Taught to Athletes*

In hockey culture, the priority is clear. Get better. Win games. Be a good teammate. Everything else is secondary. Financial education rarely fits into that environment. Not because coaches do not care, but because time and attention are limited. There are always more drills to run, more video to watch, more systems to learn.

Money also feels like a future problem. For younger players, it seems distant and abstract. For older players, it feels uncomfortable or distracting. The result is the same. Most athletes leave the game without ever being taught how money actually works.

In hockey terms, it is like being taught how to skate, shoot, pass, and defend, but never being shown how to manage your energy over a full season. You might look fine early. But eventually, the cracks show.

When athletes do not get formal education, they fill the gap with assumptions. That is where confusion starts.

## *Money Myths Passed Through Locker Rooms*

Every locker room has stories. Someone knows a guy who bought real estate and got rich fast. Someone else talks about a big stock win. Someone jokes that debt is normal because everyone has it. These comments are usually casual, not malicious, but they shape beliefs.

Common myths sound like this:

If you make more money, money problems disappear.

Investing is just educated gambling.

You have to take big risks to get ahead.

Saving means you are playing scared.

In hockey, that would be like believing you need a highlight-reel goal every shift to matter. That is not how games are won. Coaches value players who are reliable, positionally sound, and consistent. Flash without fundamentals gets exposed quickly.

Financial myths work the same way. They exaggerate outcomes and ignore process. They make money feel unpredictable and emotional instead of systematic and learnable.

## *Saving vs Investing vs Gambling*

One of the biggest sources of confusion is not understanding the difference between saving, investing, and gambling. They get lumped together, even though they serve very different purposes.

Saving is about protection. It is money set aside for short-term needs and unexpected events. Think of it as defensive hockey. You are not trying to score. You are preventing damage. Emergency funds, cash reserves, and short-term savings keep one bad bounce from turning into a season-ending injury.

Investing is about long-term growth. It is about positioning yourself to benefit from time, discipline, and compounding. This is like playing a full season. You trust systems. You accept ups and downs. You focus on process over single games.

Gambling is chasing outcomes without a plan. It relies on emotion, timing, and luck. In hockey terms, it is forcing cross-ice passes through traffic every shift and hoping one gets through. Occasionally it works. Over time, it leads to turnovers.

When athletes confuse these categories, money feels chaotic. They save too little, invest without understanding, and gamble without admitting it. The confusion is not about intelligence. It is about missing definitions.

## *Why Consistency Beats Chasing Big Plays*

Hockey players know this lesson, even if they forget to apply it to money. Games are rarely won by one massive hit or one desperate shot. They are won by teams that win board battles, manage the puck, and stay disciplined shift after shift.

Financial progress works the same way.

Chasing big plays looks exciting. Trying to double money quickly. Jumping into whatever is hot. Making emotional decisions based on recent results. It feels active. It feels aggressive. But it is exhausting and unreliable.

Consistency, on the other hand, looks boring. Regular saving. Automatic contributions. Long-term investing. Reviewing progress occasionally instead of obsessively. That is the financial equivalent of rolling four lines and trusting the system.

Most former players struggle not because they lack opportunity, but because they apply game-night urgency to long-term decisions. Money does not reward urgency. It rewards patience.

## *Coach's Perspective*

What would your coach say if money were part of the film session?

Stop forcing plays.

Value the puck.

Do not try to win it all in one shift.

Stick to the system.

Consistency beats talent when talent gets impatient.

A coach would remind you that effort and discipline matter more than flair. That fundamentals keep you in games. That chasing highlights usually hurts the team. Financially, the same advice applies. You do not need to be perfect. You need to be consistent.

## *Game Situations and Decision Points*

Imagine two scenarios.

First, you get a bonus or unexpected income. Do you spend it immediately because you earned it, or do you assign it a role in your plan? That decision mirrors a power play. Do you force shots, or do you work the puck until the opening is real?

Second, the market drops or expenses spike. Do you panic and abandon your plan, or do you stay composed and make small adjustments? That is a third-period test of discipline.

In both cases, the outcome depends less on intelligence and more on habits.

## *Common Player Mistakes and Financial Parallels*

Players often rely on adrenaline instead of structure. Financially, that leads to impulsive decisions.

Players underestimate fatigue over a long season. Financially, that leads to burnout and inconsistency.

Players chase big moments instead of mastering details. Financially, that leads to gambling disguised as investing.

These mistakes are understandable. They come from the same competitive drive that made you successful. But unchecked, they create confusion instead of clarity.

## *Winning the Long Game*

Money feels confusing after the final buzzer because the structure that supported you disappears. The solution is not more risk or more complexity. It is rebuilding fundamentals with intention.

When you understand the difference between saving, investing, and gambling, decisions slow down. When you ignore locker-room myths and focus on systems, confidence grows. When you choose consistency over big plays, progress becomes predictable.

Hockey taught you how to win over time. This chapter is about applying that same discipline to money.

## *Athlete Takeaways*

- Stop forcing financial plays. Consistency wins more seasons than highlights
- Know your role. Saving defends, investing grows, gambling turns the puck over
- Ignore locker-room money talk and trust your own system
- Value the puck with money the same way you do on the ice
- Play the long season. One good shift repeated beats one big moment

# Chapter 2: Read the Scoreboard

## *Your Financial Snapshot*

Every hockey player learns early to check the scoreboard. Not obsessively. Not emotionally. But consistently. You need to know the score, the time left, and the situation so you can make the right decisions on the ice. A team that ignores the scoreboard plays reckless hockey. A team that panics because of it plays scared. The best teams use it as information, not judgment.

Your financial snapshot works the same way.

Most money problems do not come from a lack of effort. They come from playing blind. When you do not know what is coming in, what is going out, or where you stand overall, every decision feels stressful. You guess. You react. You hope. That is not a strategy. That is chasing the puck.

This chapter is about learning how to read your financial scoreboard so you can play with awareness instead of anxiety.

## *Opening Story From the Rink*

Think about a late second-period shift. You hop over the boards, the pace is high, and the building is loud. If you do not know whether you are up one or down one, you cannot manage risk correctly. You might force offense when patience is required. Or sit back when pressure is needed.

The scoreboard does not tell you how good you are. It tells you where you are.

Your financial snapshot serves the same purpose. It is not about judgment or shame. It is about clarity.

## *Income, Expenses, and Cash Flow*

### Where the Puck Is Moving

Cash flow is the movement of money into and out of your life. Income is money coming in. Expenses are money going out. The difference between the two determines whether you are building momentum or chasing from behind.

In hockey terms, cash flow is puck movement. If the puck is moving north more than south, you are controlling play. If it keeps coming back toward your own zone, you are under pressure.

Many players know what they make but have only a vague sense of what they spend. That gap creates problems. You cannot out-earn poor awareness forever.

Income can come from salary, bonuses, endorsements, side work, or business ownership. Expenses include everything from rent and food to subscriptions, travel, and lifestyle spending. When expenses consistently exceed income, stress builds quietly, just like long defensive-zone shifts.

Positive cash flow gives you options. Negative cash flow forces mistakes.

## *Coach's Perspective*

What would a coach say after watching your financial shifts on film?

Know your minutes.

Do not take penalties you cannot kill.

Win your shifts before trying to win the game.

If you keep getting pinned, something needs to change.

A coach would not yell about one bad shift. But they would not ignore a pattern either. Cash flow patterns matter more than any single expense.

## *Assets, Liabilities, and Net Worth*

**Who Is On the Ice With You**

Assets are things you own that have value. Cash, savings, investments, retirement accounts, and property all count. Liabilities are what you owe. Loans, credit cards, and other debts live here.

Net worth is simply assets minus liabilities.

In hockey terms, think of assets as your lineup and liabilities as the opposing forecheck. A deep, well-balanced roster gives you options. Too much pressure from liabilities limits your ability to move the puck.

Net worth is not a score of your worth as a person. It is a snapshot of positioning. Early in life, many players have low or even negative net worth. That is normal. What matters is direction. Are you building depth, or are you adding pressure?

Tracking net worth over time is like tracking goal differential across a season. One game does not define it. Trends do.

## *Fixed vs Variable Expenses*

**Your Guaranteed Shifts vs Optional Ice Time**

Fixed expenses are costs that stay relatively consistent. Rent or mortgage payments. Insurance premiums. Minimum loan payments. These are your guaranteed shifts. You cannot avoid them without making major lineup changes.

Variable expenses change month to month. Food, entertainment, travel, gear, and discretionary spending fall here. This is optional ice time. It is where adjustments are easiest.

Many players focus on cutting small variable expenses while ignoring oversized fixed commitments. That is like shortening shifts but never fixing line matchups. Both matter, but structure matters more.

Understanding the difference helps you know where you can actually make changes without burning energy on the wrong battles.

## *Film Review*

**Where Your Money Actually Goes**

Film does not lie. Neither does your bank statement.

Most athletes are shocked the first time they truly review their spending. Not because it is reckless, but because it is invisible. Small expenses repeat. Subscriptions pile up. Convenience spending becomes automatic.

A financial film review means looking back, not to criticize, but to learn tendencies. Where are you spending more than expected? Where are you spending less? Are your choices aligned with what you say matters?

This review turns emotions into information. It shows you where habits help and where they hurt.

## *Game Situations and Decision Points*

Situation one: You realize your cash flow is tighter than expected. Do you immediately panic and cut everything, or do you identify the real pressure points and adjust intentionally?

Situation two: You notice your net worth has not changed much despite decent income. Do you ignore it and hope it fixes itself, or do you examine liabilities and savings habits?

Situation three: You see variable spending creeping up each month. Do you blame discipline, or do you redesign systems?

Each choice mirrors a hockey decision. Do you force a breakout under pressure, or do you reset and support?

## *Common Player Mistakes and Financial Parallels*

Players often play fast without awareness. Financially, that looks like spending without tracking.

Players focus on effort instead of positioning. Financially, that looks like earning more instead of fixing structure.

Players avoid watching bad film. Financially, that looks like avoiding statements and balances.

Ignoring the scoreboard never improves the outcome.

### *Winning the Long Game*

Reading the scoreboard does not win games by itself. It enables smart decisions. The same is true financially. A clear snapshot does not guarantee success, but it gives you control.

When you understand cash flow, net worth, and spending patterns, you stop guessing. You start managing. That is how confidence replaces anxiety.

The best players know where they stand at all times. The best financial outcomes come from the same awareness.

### *Athlete Takeaways*

- Know the score. Awareness beats guessing every time
- Cash flow is puck movement. Control it or chase all season
- Net worth is positioning, not identity
- Fixed expenses set your shifts. Variable expenses are where you adjust
- Watch the film. Patterns decide outcomes, not one bad play

# Chapter 3: Playing the Forecheck

## *Budgeting and Saving*

Good hockey teams do not wait for chances to fall into their lap. They create pressure. They establish the forecheck, force mistakes, and wear opponents down shift after shift. The forecheck is not flashy. It is work. It is structure. It is commitment to doing the same hard things over and over until momentum turns in your favor.

Budgeting and saving work the same way.

Most athletes do not struggle financially because they lack income. They struggle because there is no system applying pressure to their money. Without a forecheck, money drifts wherever it wants. With one, you control pace, limit mistakes, and set up long-term scoring opportunities.

This chapter is about building a budgeting and saving system that works the way a great forecheck works: consistent, disciplined, and relentless.

## *Opening Story From the Rink*

Think about a team that wants to play fast but never commits to the forecheck. Defensemen break out clean. Neutral-zone play is easy. Eventually, your team is stuck defending instead of attacking.

Now think about a team that forechecks with purpose. First player in sets the angle. Second player supports. Third player stays high. Nothing looks dramatic on one shift, but by the third period, the other team is tired, rushed, and mistake-prone.

Budgeting works the same way. One month of discipline does not change your life. Systems applied over time do.

## *Budgeting Systems That Actually Work*

### Setting the Forecheck Structure

A budget is not a punishment. It is a game plan. It tells your money where to go before it disappears.

The biggest mistake athletes make with budgeting is trying to micromanage every dollar. That is like trying to forecheck without roles. It becomes exhausting and unsustainable.

Effective budgeting systems share a few traits:

They are simple.

They are repeatable.

They focus on big categories, not every detail.

Some players use a percentage-based system. Income gets split into buckets like spending, saving, and investing. Others prefer a fixed-expense-first approach where essentials are covered, savings are automated, and the rest is discretionary.

The best system is the one you can run even during busy seasons.

In hockey terms, your budget sets your forecheck lanes. You decide ahead of time where pressure is applied and where space is allowed. Without that structure, money slips through the neutral zone untouched.

## *Coach's Perspective*

What would your coach say about your financial forecheck?

Win your battles early.

Do not chase after the puck late.

Everyone has a role.

Effort is non-negotiable.

A coach would remind you that forechecking is about habits, not heroics.

Budgeting is the same. You do not need perfection. You need consistency.

## *Automating Savings*

### Daily Reps That Add Up

No one gets stronger from one workout. Strength comes from reps done consistently, even when motivation is low.

Saving works the same way.

Automation turns saving into a habit instead of a decision. When money is moved automatically into savings or investment accounts, discipline happens before temptation shows up.

This is the financial version of showing up to practice every day. You do not ask yourself if you feel like it. You do it because it is scheduled.

Automating savings accomplishes three things:

It removes emotion from the decision.

It creates consistency.

It builds momentum quietly.

Many athletes try to save whatever is left at the end of the month. That is like hoping to forecheck after the puck is already gone. Paying yourself first is how pressure gets established.

## *Emergency Funds*

### Injury Protection for Your Finances

Every hockey player understands the risk of injury. You stretch. You condition. You wear protection. Not because you plan to get hurt, but because you plan to keep playing if something happens.

An emergency fund is financial injury protection.

It is money set aside for unexpected events: medical bills, car repairs, job disruptions, or family emergencies. Without it, one bad hit can derail everything.

Emergency funds prevent small problems from becoming career-altering mistakes. They keep you from relying on credit cards, loans, or panic decisions.

In hockey terms, an emergency fund is your depth and medical staff combined. It keeps you in the game while you recover.

Most players aim for a few months of essential expenses. That target matters less than starting and building steadily. Like conditioning, you improve over time.

## *Balancing Lifestyle With Long-Term Wins*

**Playing the Full Season**

Hockey seasons are long. Teams that burn out early rarely finish strong. Smart teams manage energy, minutes, and expectations.

Financially, the same principle applies.

Extreme restriction does not work long term. Neither does reckless spending. The goal is balance: enjoying life today without stealing too much from tomorrow.

A good budget includes room for enjoyment. Meals out. Travel. Experiences. Those matter. But they are planned, not impulsive.

This is the difference between controlled aggression and undisciplined play. One leads to goals. The other leads to penalties.

When lifestyle spending is aligned with your values and plan, guilt disappears. You know you are playing your shifts responsibly.

## *Game Situations and Decision Points*

Situation one: You get a raise or bonus. Do you immediately increase spending, or do you adjust savings first and then upgrade intentionally?

Situation two: An unexpected expense hits. Do you rely on your emergency fund, or do you put it on a card and hope it works out?

Situation three: You feel restricted by your budget. Do you abandon it entirely, or do you adjust categories to make it sustainable?

Each situation mirrors a forechecking decision. Do you stay disciplined, or do you abandon structure under pressure?

## *Common Player Mistakes and Financial Parallels*

Players often skate hard without purpose. Financially, that looks like budgeting without automation.

Players chase hits instead of positioning. Financially, that looks like cutting small expenses while ignoring big leaks.

Players skip conditioning and expect results. Financially, that looks like saving inconsistently and hoping timing fixes it.

Winning teams respect systems.

## *Winning the Long Game*

Budgeting and saving do not feel exciting in the moment. Neither does a well-executed forecheck. But over time, they tilt the ice.

When your money is structured, automated, and protected, stress drops. Options increase. Confidence grows.

You stop reacting and start controlling play.

That is how championships are built. One disciplined shift at a time.

## *Athlete Takeaways*

- A budget is a game plan, not a restriction
- Automation turns saving into daily reps
- Emergency funds keep one bad hit from ending your season
- Balance lifestyle and discipline to last the full year
- Forecheck your money early or spend the game chasing

# Chapter 4: Credit, Debt, and Playing Through Contact

Hockey is not a non-contact sport. Every player knows that. You will get hit. You will get leaned on. You will have to play through contact if you want to stay on the ice. The difference between players who last and players who break down is not whether contact happens. It is how they absorb it, manage it, and recover from it.

Credit and debt work the same way.

You will almost certainly use credit at some point in your life. A car. An apartment. A home. Maybe school or business expenses. Credit itself is not the enemy. Poor positioning, bad decisions, and panic under pressure are.

This chapter is about learning how to play through financial contact without letting debt shorten your career.

## *Opening Story From the Rink*

Think about a rookie who goes into the corner with his head down. He might get the puck once or twice, but eventually the hits pile up. Injuries follow. Confidence drops. Minutes disappear.

Now think about a veteran who expects contact. He keeps his feet moving. He protects the puck. He knows when to absorb the hit and when to move it quickly. Same rink. Same contact. Very different outcomes.

Debt works the same way. Used without awareness, it crushes you. Used intentionally, it becomes manageable friction, not career-ending damage.

## *How Credit Scores and Reports Work*

**Your Reputation on the Ice**

A credit score is not a moral judgment. It is a reputation score. It tells lenders how reliable you have been at honoring your commitments.

In hockey terms, your credit score is your trust level with the coaching staff. Do you get the benefit of the doubt, or are you glued to the bench after one mistake?

Credit scores are built from a few main components:

Payment history. Did you pay on time?

Amounts owed. How much of your available credit are you using?

Length of history. How long have you been playing this game?

New credit. Are you constantly changing lines?

Credit mix. Can you handle different roles responsibly?

The most important factor is payment history. Missed payments are like repeated turnovers in your own zone. They stay on the film for a long time.

Your credit report is the full game tape. It shows accounts, balances, payment behavior, and any negative events. Reviewing it regularly is like watching film on yourself. You cannot fix what you refuse to see.

## *Coach's Perspective*

A coach would be blunt here.

Protect the puck.

Know the situation.

Do not beat yourself.

Availability matters.

Your coach would remind you that talent does not matter if you are always in the penalty box. Credit mistakes are self-inflicted penalties that compound over time.

## *Credit Cards, Loans, and Interest*

### Understanding the Contact

Credit cards and loans are tools. Tools can help or hurt depending on how you use them.

A credit card is short-term borrowing with very high interest if you carry balances. It is designed for convenience, not long-term financing. Treating a credit card like extra income is like trying to skate through three defenders instead of making the simple pass.

Loans are longer-term obligations. Car loans, student loans, personal loans, and mortgages all have different terms, rates, and risks. The common thread is interest.

Interest is the cost of borrowing. It is the price you pay for playing through contact instead of avoiding it. The higher the interest rate, the harder the hit.

Many athletes underestimate interest because it feels invisible. Small balances grow quietly. Minimum payments give a false sense of control. Over time, interest becomes the opponent that never gets tired.

Understanding interest is understanding the physics of the game. Ignore it, and it will dominate you.

## *Good Debt vs Bad Debt*

### Positioning Matters

Not all debt is equal.

Good debt is usually tied to long-term value, reasonable rates, and a clear plan. Examples might include education that increases earning potential, or a home purchased within your means.

Bad debt is typically high-interest, consumption-based, and driven by impulse. Credit card balances for lifestyle spending. Loans taken without a plan. Financing depreciating assets beyond your budget.

In hockey terms, good debt is taking contact to make a smart play. Bad debt is taking contact for no reason and losing possession anyway.

The key difference is control. Good debt fits into a system. Bad debt forces you to react.

## *Debt Traps That Shorten Careers*

**When Contact Becomes Damage**

Some debt patterns are especially dangerous for athletes and former athletes.

Lifestyle inflation is a major one. Income increases, spending increases faster, and debt fills the gap. This is like playing top-line minutes without conditioning. It works briefly, then collapses.

Minimum-payment thinking is another trap. Paying only the minimum feels manageable but keeps you locked in the zone. You are not advancing the puck. You are just surviving shifts.

Using debt to cover cash flow problems is also a warning sign. If expenses consistently exceed income, debt becomes a crutch. Over time, it limits flexibility and options.

Finally, emotional borrowing is a silent killer. Spending to cope with stress, identity loss, or comparison often shows up after the uniform comes off. The bill arrives long after the feeling fades.

These traps shorten financial careers the same way poor habits shorten playing careers.

## *Game Situations and Decision Points*

Situation one: You want something now but do not have cash. Do you wait, adjust, or borrow without a plan?

Situation two: You carry a balance month to month. Do you increase payments aggressively or accept interest as normal?

Situation three: Your income drops or changes. Do you adjust lifestyle quickly or try to maintain appearances with debt?

Each decision mirrors a moment on the ice. Do you protect yourself and the puck, or do you expose both under pressure?

## *Common Player Mistakes and Financial Parallels*

Players try to power through hits instead of moving the puck. Financially, that looks like using credit instead of adjusting spending.

Players ignore conditioning until injuries appear. Financially, that looks like ignoring debt until it becomes overwhelming.

Players chase ice time without fundamentals. Financially, that looks like chasing lifestyle without stability.

The game punishes shortcuts.

## *Winning the Long Game*

Credit is not something to fear. It is something to respect.

When used intentionally, credit can support progress. When used emotionally or carelessly, it limits freedom.

The goal is not to avoid all contact. The goal is to stay upright, available, and effective over a long season.

That means knowing your numbers. Paying on time. Reducing high-interest balances. Borrowing only with a plan. And never confusing credit with income.

Championship players stay on the ice because they play smart through contact.

## *Athlete Takeaways*

- Credit is reputation. Protect it like ice time
- Interest is contact that adds up over shifts
- Good debt supports the game plan, bad debt forces panic
- Minimum payments keep you trapped in your zone
- Play through contact, but do not let it end your season

# Chapter 5: The Locker Room of Money

*Banking Basics*

Every team has a locker room. It is not glamorous, but it is essential. It is where preparation happens, where routines are built, and where the work that never shows up on the highlight reel actually matters.

Your banking system is your financial locker room.

If it is disorganized, rushed, or ignored, everything else suffers. If it is clean, intentional, and well-run, the rest of your financial game becomes easier to execute.

This chapter is about understanding the basic banking tools that support every other money decision you make, the same way a locker room supports every shift you take.

*Opening Story From the Rink*

Think about showing up to the rink on game day and nothing is where it should be. Your skates are missing. Your gloves are wet. Tape is gone. Nobody knows where the extra sticks are.

You might still play, but you are distracted, rushed, and frustrated before the puck even drops.

That is how many people operate financially. Their money is scattered. Bills are unpredictable. Transfers feel confusing. When pressure hits, mistakes follow.

A good locker room does not win games by itself, but a bad one can absolutely lose them.

## *Checking vs Savings Accounts*

**Different Rooms, Different Purposes**

A checking account is your bench. It is where money flows in and out constantly. Paychecks land here. Bills leave from here. This account is built for movement, not storage.

A savings account is more like the training room or equipment storage. It is where resources are protected and set aside for future use. Emergency funds. Short-term goals. Planned expenses.

Problems happen when athletes confuse the two.

Keeping everything in checking leads to overspending. Seeing a large balance creates a false sense of availability, just like leaving extra sticks on the bench invites careless use.

Using savings like checking defeats its purpose. Pulling money in and out constantly disrupts discipline and increases the chance of impulse decisions.

The separation matters. Checking is for operations. Savings is for protection and preparation.

## *Coach's Perspective*

A coach would be clear.

Know your role.

Put things where they belong.

Do not mix responsibilities.

Details matter.

Your coach would not let defensemen drift into random assignments. Your money needs the same structure.

## *Online Banks vs Traditional Banks*

**Different Facilities, Same Game**

Traditional banks are like older rinks. Brick-and-mortar locations. In-person service. Familiar systems. For some people, that physical presence provides comfort and accountability.

Online banks are like modern training facilities. Fewer buildings, more efficiency. Lower overhead. Often higher interest rates on savings and fewer fees.

Neither is automatically better. The key question is fit.

If you value face-to-face interaction, cash deposits, or local relationships, a traditional bank may work well. If you prioritize simplicity, automation, and higher yields on savings, online banks often excel.

Many players use both. A traditional checking account for day-to-day needs and an online savings account for emergency funds and longer-term goals.

In hockey terms, it is not about the building. It is about whether the facility supports how you train and prepare.

## *How Money Moves Electronically*

**The Passing Game**

Money rarely moves as cash anymore. It moves electronically through systems that act like passing lanes.

Direct deposit is a clean breakout. Paychecks arrive automatically without effort.

Electronic bill pay is a controlled zone exit. Scheduled, predictable, and repeatable.

Transfers between accounts are like line changes. They need to be timed and intentional to avoid chaos.

Peer-to-peer apps are quick touch passes. Useful in the right moment, risky if overused or unsecured.

Problems arise when athletes do not understand where the puck is moving.

Missed transfers, overdrafts, delayed payments, and duplicate subscriptions all come from lack of awareness.

Watching your transactions regularly is film study. You learn patterns, spot mistakes, and adjust before small issues turn into big ones.

## *Protecting Yourself From Fraud and Overdrafts*

**Defensive Responsibility**

Every player has defensive responsibility, even scorers. Banking is no different.

Fraud is an opponent that looks for lazy coverage. Weak passwords. Ignored alerts. Shared information.

Strong defense includes:

Unique, secure passwords

Two-factor authentication

Account alerts for large transactions

Regular review of statements

Overdrafts are self-inflicted penalties. They happen when spending exceeds awareness. Fees pile up quietly, like penalty minutes that do not show up until the game slips away.

Simple systems prevent most overdrafts. Keeping a buffer in checking. Linking savings as backup. Turning on alerts when balances drop.

Good defense is boring. It does not get applause. It keeps you in the game.

## *Game Situations and Decision Points*

Situation one: You keep all your money in one account. Do you separate roles or accept ongoing confusion?

Situation two: You notice small fees each month. Do you investigate or ignore them?

Situation three: You rarely review transactions. Do you start film study or wait until a mistake costs you?

Each choice affects execution before the game even starts.

### *Common Player Mistakes and Financial Parallels*

Players show up late to meetings. Financially, that looks like missed payments and overdrafts.

Players ignore defensive assignments. Financially, that looks like fraud exposure and weak security.

Players rely on talent without structure. Financially, that looks like income without systems.

The basics are not optional.

### *Winning the Long Game*

Banking is not about maximizing returns. It is about minimizing mistakes and creating stability.

A clean locker room leads to better preparation. Clear systems reduce stress. Predictable routines protect energy and focus.

When your banking foundation is solid, everything else becomes easier. Budgeting sticks. Saving becomes automatic. Investing decisions improve because cash flow is under control.

Winning with money one shift at a time starts here.

### *Athlete Takeaways*

- Your bank accounts are your locker room, keep them organized
- Checking is for movement, savings is for protection
- Automation is clean puck movement, chaos creates turnovers
- Fraud and overdrafts are defensive breakdowns
- Strong fundamentals keep you available for the full season

# Part II: Defense, Goaltending, and Protection

If you cannot protect the net, nothing else matters.

Every hockey player learns this early.

You can have elite scorers, a fast transition game, and highlight reel goals, but if you cannot protect the net, the season falls apart. Defensive structure and goaltending do not show up on stat sheets the way goals do, but they decide outcomes over time. Championships are rarely won by the team with the flashiest offense. They are won by the teams that make it hard to score against.

Money works the same way.

Part II of this book is about protection. Not growth. Not upside. Protection. It is about managing risk, guarding against setbacks, and making sure one bad bounce does not undo years of work.

Most financial damage does not come from bad investing. It comes from unprotected risk.

Why Protection Comes Before Offense

In hockey, you do not ask your goalie to score. You ask them to keep the puck out of the net. Their job is to absorb pressure so the team can stay composed and play its game.

Financial protection plays the same role. Insurance, risk awareness, and contingency planning exist so that one injury, accident, lawsuit, or unexpected event does not wipe out your progress. They create stability under pressure. They allow you to stay in control when things go wrong.

Athletes often underestimate this phase because it feels passive. It does not feel like progress. It feels like paying for something you hope never happens.

That is exactly why it matters.

You do not notice good defense when it is working. You only notice it when it fails.

Risk Is Always on the Ice

Every shift carries risk. You accept that because it is part of the game. A bad bounce, a missed assignment, an awkward collision. You cannot remove risk from hockey. You learn to manage it.

Financial life is the same.

Income changes. Health issues happen. Cars break down. Markets fluctuate. People make mistakes. Lawsuits happen. None of this is rare. It is normal.

The goal is not to eliminate risk. The goal is to manage it intelligently.

Good teams know when to pressure and when to collapse. Good financial plans know when to take risk and when to protect. Part II helps you understand where risk shows up in your life and how to guard against the kinds of losses that derail seasons.

Defense Is a System, Not a Star

Great defensive teams are not built around one player. They are built around systems. Positioning. Communication. Trust. Everyone doing their job.

Financial protection works the same way.

Health insurance protects against medical costs.

Auto and home insurance protect property.

Disability insurance protects income.

Life insurance protects dependents.

Liability coverage protects assets from lawsuits.

None of these are exciting on their own. Together, they create stability. They form a system that keeps one problem from turning into five.

Relying on one form of protection is like relying on one defenseman to stop every rush. Eventually, something gets through.

This section is about building a defensive system that holds up over time.

Goaltending Is About Consistency, Not Perfection

Even the best goalies give up goals. The difference is they do not let one goal turn into three.

Financial protection does not mean avoiding all loss. It means limiting damage. It means absorbing the hit without losing the game.

Insurance deductibles, coverage limits, and exclusions are like rebound control. You may absorb a shot, but you do not give up a second chance. You take the hit, reset, and keep playing.

The biggest financial mistakes often happen after an initial setback. Panic. Overreaction. Scrambling for cash. Liquidating investments at the worst time.

Good protection keeps you calm so you can make clear decisions under pressure.

Why Athletes Are Especially Vulnerable

Athletes face unique risk profiles.

Income can be uneven or short lived. Bodies are income producing assets. Public exposure increases liability. Career transitions happen earlier than expected. One injury can change everything.

Many athletes assume protection can wait until later. That is usually when it is too late or far more expensive.

Part II is not about fear. It is about realism.

You trained for worst case scenarios on the ice. You practiced defensive drills you hoped you would not need. Financial protection is the same mindset applied to life.

The Cost of Ignoring Defense

Teams that ignore defense burn out goalies, shorten careers, and waste talent.

Financially, ignoring protection leads to:

Debt replacing savings

Insurance gaps creating long term damage

Stress replacing focus

Short term fixes creating permanent problems

None of that comes from bad intentions. It comes from lack of structure.

How This Section Fits Into the Bigger Plan

Part I built your foundation. Income awareness. Cash flow. Banking systems.

Part II protects that foundation.

Only after protection is in place does it make sense to push offense, build wealth, and take calculated risks. That is why investing comes later in the book.

You do not push the pace until you trust your defense.

A Coach's Reminder

A coach would not sugarcoat it.

You cannot win trading chances all night.

Protect the middle.

Trust the system.

Stay disciplined.

That advice applies to money just as much as hockey.

What Comes Next

The chapters ahead will break down:

How to think about risk without fear

How insurance actually works in plain language

How to avoid the most common coverage mistakes athletes make

How to protect income, assets, and future options

This is not about playing scared.

It is about staying in the game long enough to win.

Protect the net first. Everything else follows.

# Chapter 6: Risk Awareness and Smart Decision Making

**Knowing When to Press and When to Clear the Puck**

Every hockey player has lived this moment.

You are pinned in your own zone. The crowd is loud. The forecheck is heavy. You see a risky breakout pass through the middle that could spring a rush the other way. You also see the safe option. Glass and out. No highlight. No applause. Just survival.

Great players know the difference.

This chapter is about learning that same instinct with money. Risk is always present. The mistake is not taking risk. The mistake is taking the wrong risk at the wrong time for the wrong reason.

## *Opening Shift: When a Bad Decision Changes Momentum*

Momentum shifts in hockey rarely come from talent gaps. They come from decision-making.

One careless turnover leads to extended zone time. One forced play leads to a goal against. Suddenly a tied game becomes a chase.

Financial momentum works the same way. One rushed decision. One emotional reaction. One misunderstood risk. The damage does not always show up immediately, but it changes the game state.

Risk awareness is about reading the ice before the puck ever touches your stick.

## *Emotional Risk vs Financial Risk*

Not all risk is the same.

**Emotional risk** is how a decision feels. Fear. Excitement. Pressure. Confidence. Ego.

**Financial risk** is the actual likelihood and impact of loss over time.

Athletes are trained to manage physical risk. You understand angles. Speed. Contact. But money introduces emotional risk in unfamiliar ways.

Fear makes people freeze.

Greed makes people force plays.

Confidence turns into overconfidence.

In hockey terms, emotional risk is panic during a long shift. Financial risk is whether the play actually makes sense given time, score, and personnel.

Smart decisions separate how something feels from what it actually does.

## *Time Horizon Changes Everything*

Time horizon is the scoreboard.

Early in the game, you can take more chances. Late in the third, protecting a lead matters more than creating offense.

Financially, time horizon works the same way. Money you need soon should not be exposed to the same risk as money you will not touch for decades.

Short-term money is defensive zone money.

Long-term money can handle neutral zone pressure.

Athletes often make mistakes by putting short-term needs into long-term risk or long-term money into short-term panic.

Knowing your time horizon tells you how aggressive you can be without getting burned.

### *Flexibility Is a Competitive Advantage*

Good teams stay flexible. They can roll four lines. They can adjust matchups. They can respond to injuries.

Financial flexibility is just as important.

Emergency savings. Accessible cash. Low fixed costs. Insurance coverage. These give you options when things change.

Without flexibility, every setback feels like a crisis. With flexibility, you clear the puck, reset, and change lines.

Risk is not dangerous when you have room to maneuver. It becomes dangerous when you are boxed in.

### *How Risk Touches Every Money Decision*

Risk is not limited to investing.

Spending decisions carry risk.

Career choices carry risk.

Debt decisions carry risk.

Insurance choices carry risk.

Even doing nothing carries risk.

Ignoring risk does not make it disappear. It just moves it somewhere you are not looking.

In hockey, ignoring the weak-side winger does not eliminate them. It gives them a tap-in.

Financial awareness means scanning the whole ice, not just the puck.

### *Knowing When to Press*

There are moments to press.

When you have margin.

When you have support.

When the odds are in your favor.

In money terms, this might mean investing more when income is stable, savings are strong, and time horizon is long. It might mean taking career risk when skills are transferable and downside is manageable.

Pressing works when it is intentional, not emotional.

Great teams press with structure. They do not all chase the puck.

### *Knowing When to Clear the Puck*

Clearing the puck is underrated.

It is not quitting. It is survival.

Financially, clearing the puck might mean paying down high-interest debt before investing aggressively. It might mean holding cash during uncertain transitions. It might mean saying no to an opportunity that looks exciting but threatens stability.

Clearing the puck buys time. Time to reset. Time to change lines. Time to regain position.

Winning seasons are built on thousands of smart clears that never make highlight reels.

### *Coach's Perspective: What Would Your Coach Say?*

A coach would be blunt.

Know the situation.

Read the ice.

Stop forcing plays.

Live to fight the next shift.

They would remind you that discipline wins games long before talent shows up.

Risk management is not passive. It is intentional restraint.

### *Game Situations and Decision Points*

**Situation 1:** You just got a bonus or signing check. Do you chase upside immediately or secure your base first?

Financial lesson: Pressing without protection exposes you to unnecessary loss.

**Situation 2:** Markets drop and everyone is panicking. Do you abandon the plan or stay disciplined?

Financial lesson: Emotional risk is loud. Long-term risk is quiet.

**Situation 3:** You are unhappy in a job but financially stretched. Do you quit without a plan or build flexibility first?

Financial lesson: Timing matters more than impulse.

### *Common Athlete Mistakes and Financial Parallels*

Athletes trust confidence too much.

Financially, that becomes overexposure.

Athletes hate playing safe.

Financially, that becomes reckless risk-taking.

Athletes chase momentum.

Financially, that leads to buying high and selling low.

The game punishes impatience.

### *Winning the Long Game*

Championship teams are not fearless. They are disciplined.

They know when to press.

They know when to protect.

They know that one bad decision can erase ten good ones.

Financial success works the same way. Risk is not something to avoid. It is something to manage with awareness, timing, and structure.

The goal is not to win every shift.

The goal is to still be standing at the end of the season.

*Athlete Takeaways*

- Read the ice before you make money decisions
- Separate emotional pressure from real financial risk
- Time horizon determines how aggressive you can play
- Flexibility gives you options under pressure
- Clearing the puck is sometimes the smartest play

# Chapter 7: Insurance Fundamentals Every Player Needs

**Protecting the Net Before the Shot Ever Happens**

Every hockey player understands one truth early.

You can dominate possession. You can win faceoffs. You can generate offense all night. None of it matters if you cannot protect the net.

Insurance plays that exact role in your financial life.

It is not exciting. It does not score goals. You hope it never becomes the star of the game. But when something goes wrong, insurance is what keeps one bad bounce from turning into a season-ending loss.

This chapter is about understanding insurance as defensive structure, not paperwork.

## *Opening Shift: When Defense Fails, Everything Else Collapses*

Think about a team with no defensive discipline.

Defensemen chase hits. Forwards cheat for offense. The goalie faces odd-man rushes all night. Even elite talent cannot survive long.

Financially, skipping insurance creates the same chaos. One accident. One injury. One lawsuit. One unexpected event. Suddenly years of progress disappear.

Insurance does not prevent bad things from happening. It prevents bad things from ending the game.

## *Health Insurance: Your First Line of Defense*

Health insurance is the most immediate form of protection most athletes need.

In hockey terms, this is your goaltender.

Injuries happen. Illness happens. Recovery costs money. Without coverage, even a routine medical issue can create financial stress that lingers for years.

Health insurance helps cover doctor visits, hospital stays, prescriptions, and preventive care. Plans vary widely, but the goal is the same. Limit catastrophic damage.

Key concepts matter.

Premiums are what you pay every month to keep coverage active.

Deductibles are what you pay before insurance starts sharing costs.

Copays and coinsurance are your share after coverage kicks in.

Higher deductibles often mean lower premiums. Lower deductibles usually mean higher premiums. Neither is automatically better. The right choice depends on health, income, and cash reserves.

Playing without health insurance is like pulling the goalie in the first period. It might save money short term. It usually ends badly.

## *Auto and Renters Insurance: Protecting the Zone*

Auto and renters insurance protect you from damage and liability tied to everyday life.

Auto insurance covers accidents, injuries, and damage involving your vehicle. Renters insurance protects your personal property and provides liability coverage if someone gets hurt in your space.

In hockey terms, this is team defense. Everyone has a role.

Auto insurance is required in most places, but minimum coverage is rarely enough. Liability matters more than repairing your own car. Medical claims and lawsuits are what create long-term damage.

Renters insurance is often overlooked because it feels optional. It is not. It covers theft, fire, water damage, and liability, often for a very low cost.

Not having renters insurance is like leaving the slot wide open because you assumed nothing would happen there.

### *Homeowners Insurance: Defending the Blue Paint*

Homeowners insurance is heavier coverage for a bigger asset.

It protects the structure, your belongings, and your liability exposure as a property owner. It also adds complexity.

Homes face risks from fire, storms, water damage, theft, and injury claims. Repairs are expensive. Legal exposure can be significant.

In hockey terms, this is protecting the crease. You do not get casual here.

Coverage limits need to reflect real replacement costs, not what you paid for the home. Liability limits should be high enough to protect your net worth, not just satisfy a lender.

Homeownership increases responsibility. Insurance keeps that responsibility from becoming overwhelming.

### *Deductibles, Premiums, and Coverage Limits Explained*

Insurance decisions always involve tradeoffs.

Premiums are guaranteed costs.

Deductibles are conditional costs.

Coverage limits define how much protection you actually have.

Higher deductibles lower premiums but require cash on hand when something happens. Lower deductibles raise premiums but reduce out-of-pocket shock.

Coverage limits are often the most misunderstood. Being insured does not automatically mean being protected. If limits are too low, you are still exposed.

In hockey terms, this is personnel usage. You cannot play your fourth line against the opponent's top unit and hope it works.

The structure has to match the situation.

## *Why Athletes Commonly Get This Wrong*

Athletes are used to managing physical risk, not financial risk.

They assume youth equals safety.

They underestimate liability.

They focus on price instead of protection.

Many athletes also move frequently, changing teams, cities, apartments, and jobs. Coverage lapses happen easily during transitions.

Insurance gaps often appear during life changes. New job. New city. New car. New home. New family.

Defense breaks down when communication stops.

## *Coach's Perspective: What Would Your Coach Say?*

A coach would not sugarcoat it.

Protect the net.

Know your assignments.

Do not take shortcuts on defense.

Everyone is responsible.

They would remind you that championships are built on fundamentals, not highlights.

Insurance is a fundamental.

## *Game Situations and Decision Points*

**Situation 1:** You are young and healthy. Do you choose the cheapest health plan or one that protects against real injury risk?

Financial lesson: Injury risk does not care about age.

**Situation 2:** You rent and think you do not own much. Do you skip renters insurance or protect yourself anyway?

Financial lesson: Liability matters more than stuff.

**Situation 3:** You buy a home and accept minimum coverage to save money. Do you review limits or assume it is enough?

Financial lesson: Being underinsured is not protection.

## *Common Athlete Mistakes and Financial Parallels*

Athletes play through pain.

Financially, that becomes ignoring risk.

Athletes trust toughness.

Financially, that becomes overconfidence.

Athletes focus on offense.

Financially, that leads to defensive gaps.

Insurance mistakes rarely show up until it is too late to fix them.

## *Winning the Long Game*

Great teams defend first.

They understand that offense wins games, but defense wins seasons. Insurance is not about fear. It is about durability.

When protection is in place, you can play freely. Take opportunities. Build momentum. Recover from setbacks.

When protection is missing, every hit feels dangerous.

The goal is not to eliminate risk.

The goal is to survive it.

## *Athlete Takeaways*

- Insurance is your financial defense, not a luxury
- Health coverage protects against season-ending injuries
- Auto and renters insurance cover everyday risk and liability
- Coverage limits matter more than price alone
- Protect the net so one bad bounce does not end the season

# Chapter 8: Life, Disability, and Liability Coverage

**Protecting Your Career, Your Teammates, and the Season Ahead**

Every hockey player knows there are hits you can skate away from and hits that change everything.

Some injuries sideline you for a shift. Others end seasons. A few end careers. The difference is not toughness. It is preparation and protection.

Life, disability, and liability insurance exist for the same reason teams carry depth, play disciplined defense, and protect their stars. These tools are not about pessimism. They are about continuity. They make sure one bad moment does not wipe out everything you have built.

This chapter is about protecting the engine of your financial life: your ability to earn, provide, and move forward.

## *Opening Shift: One Injury Changes the Entire Season*

Picture this.

A top-line player is having a career year. Minutes are up. Confidence is high. Then a knee injury happens along the boards. No cheap shot. No dirty play. Just hockey.

Suddenly the lineup changes. The power play adjusts. Expectations shift.

Now imagine the same moment in real life. An injury, illness, or accident limits your ability to work. Income drops or stops. Bills keep coming. Plans unravel.

Life and disability insurance exist for this exact scenario.

You do not plan for injuries because you expect them. You plan because they happen.

### *Term vs Permanent Life Insurance: Knowing the Role*

Life insurance protects the people who depend on your income.

In hockey terms, life insurance is about protecting the team when a key player is gone.

Term life insurance is simple. It provides coverage for a specific period, such as 10, 20, or 30 years. If something happens during that term, the policy pays a benefit to your beneficiaries.

Permanent life insurance lasts for your lifetime and includes additional features, such as cash value. It is more complex and more expensive.

For most players and young families, term insurance does the job. It covers the high-risk years. Mortgages. Children. Dependents. Business obligations.

Permanent insurance can have a role in advanced planning, but it is not a default choice.

In hockey terms, term insurance is a reliable defensive pairing. Permanent insurance is a specialty player. You use it intentionally, not automatically.

Buying life insurance without understanding the role is like dressing a player without knowing the system.

### *Disability Insurance: Protecting Your Most Valuable Asset*

If life insurance protects your family, disability insurance protects you.

Your ability to earn income is your most valuable financial asset. It pays for everything else. Retirement. Housing. Investing. Insurance itself.

Disability insurance replaces a portion of your income if you cannot work due to injury or illness.

In hockey terms, this is protecting your top-line center. Without them, the entire system changes.

Many athletes assume disability will not happen to them. That assumption is dangerous. Disabilities are more likely than death during working years, and many are caused by everyday injuries or illness, not catastrophic events.

Employer-provided disability coverage is often limited. Individual policies can fill gaps.

Important details matter.

How much income is replaced.

How long benefits last.

What qualifies as a disability.

The goal is continuity. Keeping cash flow alive while you recover or adjust.

Playing without disability coverage is like relying on one goalie for an entire season with no backup.

### *Umbrella Liability Coverage: Extra Protection Above the Play*

Umbrella insurance provides additional liability coverage on top of auto, renters, or homeowners policies.

It protects against large claims and lawsuits that exceed standard limits.

In hockey terms, this is support defense. When coverage breaks down, someone is there to clean it up.

As income and net worth grow, liability exposure grows too. Lawsuits do not care about intentions. Accidents happen. Claims escalate.

Umbrella coverage is usually inexpensive relative to the protection it provides. It exists for low-probability, high-impact events.

Most players never think about liability until it shows up in the form of legal action.

At that point, it is too late to add protection.

### *Common Insurance Mistakes Players Make*

Athletes make predictable mistakes around insurance.

They assume youth equals invincibility.

They buy based on price instead of protection.

They rely entirely on employer benefits.

They fail to update coverage as life changes.

Another common mistake is avoiding the conversation altogether because it feels uncomfortable.

Ignoring risk does not eliminate it.

In hockey terms, this is ignoring the defensive zone because offense feels better.

The game always comes back to fundamentals.

## *Coach's Perspective: What Would Your Coach Say?*

A coach would not hesitate.

Protect your teammates.

Know your role.

Do not leave gaps.

Prepare for adversity.

They would remind you that discipline off the puck matters just as much as skill with it.

Insurance is discipline.

It does not make headlines. It keeps you in the game.

## *Game Situations and Decision Points*

**Situation 1:** You are single and healthy. Do you skip life insurance or plan ahead for future responsibilities?

Financial lesson: Planning early lowers cost and increases options.

**Situation 2:** You rely on employer disability coverage. Do you assume it is enough or review the details?

Financial lesson: Gaps are common and expensive.

**Situation 3:** Your income increases. Do you adjust liability coverage or leave limits unchanged?

Financial lesson: Exposure grows with success.

Each decision is about protecting progress, not predicting disaster.

## *Why These Coverages Work Together*

Life, disability, and liability insurance are a system.

Life insurance protects dependents.

Disability insurance protects income.

Liability insurance protects assets.

Skipping one weakens the whole structure.

In hockey terms, you need all five skaters committed. One breakdown creates a scoring chance.

## *Winning the Long Game*

Great players think beyond the next shift.

They train for durability. They manage recovery. They respect risk.

Financial durability works the same way.

Insurance does not create wealth. It preserves it. It allows recovery. It keeps your season alive when something unexpected happens.

The goal is not fear-based planning.

The goal is confidence.

When protection is in place, you can focus on performance, growth, and opportunity without constantly worrying about the downside.

That is how professionals think.

## *Athlete Takeaways*

- Life insurance protects your team when you are gone
- Disability insurance protects your income, your real MVP
- Umbrella coverage guards against rare but costly breakdowns
- Buying insurance by price instead of purpose creates gaps
- Protect the engine so one hit does not end the season

# Part III: Creating Offense (Investing Fundamentals)

If you cannot protect the net, nothing else matters.

Every hockey player learns this early.

You can have elite scorers, a fast transition game, and highlight reel goals, but if you cannot protect the net, the season falls apart. Defensive structure and goaltending do not show up on stat sheets the way goals do, but they decide outcomes over time. Championships are rarely won by the team with the flashiest offense. They are won by the teams that make it hard to score against.

Money works the same way.

Part II of this book is about protection. Not growth. Not upside. Protection. It is about managing risk, guarding against setbacks, and making sure one bad bounce does not undo years of work.

Most financial damage does not come from bad investing. It comes from unprotected risk.

Why Protection Comes Before Offense

In hockey, you do not ask your goalie to score. You ask them to keep the puck out of the net. Their job is to absorb pressure so the team can stay composed and play its game.

Financial protection plays the same role. Insurance, risk awareness, and contingency planning exist so that one injury, accident, lawsuit, or unexpected event does not wipe out your progress. They create stability under pressure. They allow you to stay in control when things go wrong.

Athletes often underestimate this phase because it feels passive. It does not feel like progress. It feels like paying for something you hope never happens.

That is exactly why it matters.

You do not notice good defense when it is working. You only notice it when it fails.

Risk Is Always on the Ice

Every shift carries risk. You accept that because it is part of the game. A bad bounce, a missed assignment, an awkward collision. You cannot remove risk from hockey. You learn to manage it.

Financial life is the same.

Income changes. Health issues happen. Cars break down. Markets fluctuate. People make mistakes. Lawsuits happen. None of this is rare. It is normal.

The goal is not to eliminate risk. The goal is to manage it intelligently.

Good teams know when to pressure and when to collapse. Good financial plans know when to take risk and when to protect. Part II helps you understand where risk shows up in your life and how to guard against the kinds of losses that derail seasons.

Defense Is a System, Not a Star

Great defensive teams are not built around one player. They are built around systems. Positioning. Communication. Trust. Everyone doing their job.

Financial protection works the same way.

Health insurance protects against medical costs.

Auto and home insurance protect property.

Disability insurance protects income.

Life insurance protects dependents.

Liability coverage protects assets from lawsuits.

None of these are exciting on their own. Together, they create stability. They form a system that keeps one problem from turning into five.

Relying on one form of protection is like relying on one defenseman to stop every rush. Eventually, something gets through.

This section is about building a defensive system that holds up over time.

Goaltending Is About Consistency, Not Perfection

Even the best goalies give up goals. The difference is they do not let one goal turn into three.

Financial protection does not mean avoiding all loss. It means limiting damage. It means absorbing the hit without losing the game.

Insurance deductibles, coverage limits, and exclusions are like rebound control. You may absorb a shot, but you do not give up a second chance. You take the hit, reset, and keep playing.

The biggest financial mistakes often happen after an initial setback. Panic. Overreaction. Scrambling for cash. Liquidating investments at the worst time.

Good protection keeps you calm so you can make clear decisions under pressure.

Why Athletes Are Especially Vulnerable

Athletes face unique risk profiles.

Income can be uneven or short lived. Bodies are income producing assets. Public exposure increases liability. Career transitions happen earlier than expected. One injury can change everything.

Many athletes assume protection can wait until later. That is usually when it is too late or far more expensive.

Part II is not about fear. It is about realism.

You trained for worst case scenarios on the ice. You practiced defensive drills you hoped you would not need. Financial protection is the same mindset applied to life.

The Cost of Ignoring Defense

Teams that ignore defense burn out goalies, shorten careers, and waste talent.

Financially, ignoring protection leads to:

Debt replacing savings

Insurance gaps creating long term damage

Stress replacing focus

Short term fixes creating permanent problems

None of that comes from bad intentions. It comes from lack of structure.

How This Section Fits Into the Bigger Plan

Part I built your foundation. Income awareness. Cash flow. Banking systems.

Part II protects that foundation.

Only after protection is in place does it make sense to push offense, build wealth, and take calculated risks. That is why investing comes later in the book.

You do not push the pace until you trust your defense.

A Coach's Reminder

A coach would not sugarcoat it.

You cannot win trading chances all night.

Protect the middle.

Trust the system.

Stay disciplined.

That advice applies to money just as much as hockey.

What Comes Next

The chapters ahead will break down:

How to think about risk without fear

How insurance actually works in plain language

How to avoid the most common coverage mistakes athletes make

How to protect income, assets, and future options

This is not about playing scared.

It is about staying in the game long enough to win.

Protect the net first. Everything else follows.

# Chapter 9: How Financial Markets Really Work

Every hockey player remembers the moment they realized the game was faster than they thought.

The puck moved quicker. Decisions had to be made earlier. The ice felt smaller. What worked at a lower level stopped working overnight. Players who survived that jump were not always the most talented. They were the ones who understood how the game actually worked.

Financial markets have the same learning curve.

From the outside, markets look chaotic. Prices move every day. Headlines scream. Social media reacts. It feels random, emotional, and unpredictable. But just like hockey, once you understand the structure beneath the surface, the game becomes clearer. Still hard, but no longer confusing.

This chapter is about learning how the market actually plays the game so you stop reacting to noise and start making decisions like a pro.

## *Markets Are Systems, Not Slot Machines*

The biggest misunderstanding about financial markets is thinking they are casinos.

They are not.

Markets exist to allocate capital. That means connecting money with businesses, governments, and projects that need funding to grow. When you invest, you are not guessing on a score. You are participating in ownership and lending.

In hockey terms, the market is the league. It has rules, structure, and incentives. Individual games may be unpredictable, but the league itself is not random.

Short-term outcomes vary. Long-term trends reflect productivity, growth, and discipline.

Once you understand that, your mindset shifts from gambling to participation.

## *Stocks: Ownership, Not Bets*

A stock is ownership.

When you buy stock, you own a small piece of a real company. That company has employees, products, customers, expenses, and profits. Its value changes based on how well it executes over time.

In hockey terms, buying stock is committing to a team, not betting on a single shift.

Some teams grow faster. Some struggle. Some rebuild. Some dominate for years. Your return as an owner depends on long-term performance, not nightly highlights.

Athletes often struggle here because they are trained to focus on immediate results. Investing requires patience with development curves, just like prospects moving through a system.

## *Bonds: Defense and Stability*

Bonds are loans.

When you buy a bond, you are lending money to a government or company in exchange for interest and the return of your principal over time.

Bonds are not exciting. They are not meant to be.

In hockey terms, bonds are responsible defense. They do not score many goals, but they prevent disasters. They stabilize the game when things get chaotic.

Ignoring bonds entirely is like icing a roster with all forwards. It looks fun until you get burned.

## *Ownership vs Activity*

One of the biggest mistakes athletes make is confusing activity with progress.

Trading frequently feels like effort. Checking balances feels like engagement. Reacting to news feels responsible.

It is usually none of those things.

In hockey, moving your feet matters, but only if you are moving in the right direction. Skating hard in circles does not help the team.

Markets reward ownership, not constant motion. Time in the market matters more than timing the market.

## *Market Cycles Are Normal*

Markets move in cycles.

Growth periods. Slowdowns. Corrections. Recoveries. This is not a flaw. It is how systems work.

In hockey terms, seasons have momentum swings. You go on heaters. You hit slumps. You grind through stretches where nothing seems to go right. Good teams stay disciplined through all of it.

Athletes who panic during downturns often sell at the worst time. They treat a bad stretch like the season is over.

Markets reward players who stay on the bench, trust the system, and wait for their next shift.

## *Volatility Is Not the Enemy*

Volatility simply means movement.

Prices going up and down is not inherently bad. It is only dangerous when it triggers emotional decisions.

In hockey terms, volatility is pressure. Tight games. Loud buildings.

Momentum swings. Pressure does not cause mistakes. Poor responses to pressure do.

Long-term investors expect volatility. They plan for it. They build rosters that can withstand it.

Short-term thinkers let volatility dictate behavior.

## *Long-Term Strategy Beats Hot Streaks*

Hot streaks are intoxicating.

A stock doubles. A sector explodes. A friend brags about a win. Suddenly discipline feels outdated.

In hockey terms, this is chasing goals instead of playing your position.

Hot streaks rarely last. Systems do.

Long-term investing is about building a plan that fits your career stage, income, risk tolerance, and goals. Once built, that plan should not change because of headlines or hype.

Forcing offense leads to turnovers. Staying patient creates scoring chances over time.

## *Coach's Perspective*

A coach would keep it simple.

- "Play your game."
- "Trust the system."
- "Next shift."
- "Don't chase."
- "Details win games."

Markets punish players who abandon structure. They reward players who execute fundamentals under pressure.

## *Game Situations and Decision Points*

**Situation 1:**

Markets drop sharply for several months.

Do you panic and sell, or trust your long-term plan and stay invested?

**Situation 2:**

A stock or trend explodes and everyone is talking about it.

Do you chase the hot hand, or evaluate whether it fits your system?

**Situation 3:**

You feel bored because nothing dramatic is happening.

Do you create action, or respect that boring often means things are working?

Every one of these moments tests discipline more than intelligence.

## *Common Hockey Mistakes and Financial Parallels*

- **Forcing plays**
- Financially: chasing returns without understanding risk
- **Abandoning structure under pressure**
- Financially: selling during downturns
- **Playing for highlights**
- Financially: trading for excitement instead of results

The mistakes are the same. The consequences just show up later.

## *Winning the Long Game*

Markets reward patience, ownership, and discipline.

You do not need to predict the future. You need to stay invested in a system that works over time.

Just like hockey, success comes from understanding the game, respecting its structure, and executing fundamentals shift after shift.

The market does not care how hard you want to win. It responds to how well you play the long game.

## *Athlete Takeaways*

- Own the team, don't chase the puck
- Volatility is pressure, not danger
- Systems beat hot streaks
- Time on the ice matters more than flashy shifts
- Stay disciplined and trust the game plan

# Chapter 10: Risk, Return, and the Power of Compounding

Every hockey player learns this lesson early, whether they want to or not.

If you play it completely safe, you never score.

If you take reckless risks, you end up in the box or on the wrong side of the highlight reel.

Winning hockey lives in the space between caution and aggression. The same is true with money.

This chapter is about understanding risk the right way, separating normal volatility from real danger, and learning why compounding quietly wins more games than any single shift ever could.

## *Risk and Reward Are Always Linked*

There is no reward without risk.

That statement makes people uncomfortable, but it is foundational. Every meaningful opportunity carries uncertainty. The question is not whether risk exists. The question is whether the risk is intentional, understood, and appropriate.

In hockey terms, risk is pinching at the blue line.

Sometimes it leads to a goal. Sometimes it leads to a rush the other way.

Smart players do not avoid pinching entirely. They choose when to do it. They read the situation. They know who is covering behind them.

Financially, risk works the same way. Higher expected returns come with more uncertainty. Lower risk investments tend to grow more slowly. There is no free lunch.

The mistake athletes often make is swinging between extremes. Either playing too cautiously and never building momentum, or going all in on high-risk plays without a system behind them.

## *Risk Is Not the Same as Volatility*

This is one of the most misunderstood ideas in investing.

Volatility is movement.

Risk is permanent loss.

Markets go up and down. Prices fluctuate daily. That movement feels uncomfortable, especially for athletes who are wired to react instantly to feedback. But volatility alone does not destroy wealth.

In hockey terms, volatility is momentum swings.

A bad period. A tough road trip. A few unlucky bounces.

Those moments feel awful, but they do not define the season unless you let them.

Permanent loss is different. That is blowing defensive assignments repeatedly. That is taking penalties you cannot kill. That is abandoning structure entirely.

Financially, permanent loss comes from panic selling, concentrated bets, fraud, excessive leverage, or chasing returns you do not understand. Volatility hurts emotionally. Permanent loss hurts structurally.

The key is learning to tolerate normal movement without making destructive decisions.

## *Understanding Your Risk Profile*

Every player has a role.

Some play heavy minutes in high-pressure situations. Some provide stability and depth. Some are situational specialists. Teams are built intentionally, not randomly.

Your investment strategy should reflect your situation.

Career stage matters. Income stability matters. Time horizon matters. Flexibility matters.

A younger athlete with decades ahead can tolerate more volatility because recovery time exists. Someone closer to needing the money has less margin for error.

In hockey terms, you do not deploy your fourth line the same way you deploy your top line. You match risk to role.

Problems arise when people take risks that do not fit their situation. That is when panic shows up.

### *Compounding Is the Real Star*

Compounding is not exciting. That is why it works.

Compounding means your gains begin generating gains of their own. Growth builds on growth. Progress stacks quietly.

In hockey terms, compounding is development.

Extra reps in practice. Small improvements in skating. Better positioning. Smarter decisions. None of it looks dramatic day to day. Over years, it separates players.

Money works the same way. A single great year does not change a life. Consistent, disciplined investing over long periods does.

Athletes often underestimate compounding because they are conditioned to think in seasons. Financial success is built over decades.

### *Time Is the Most Powerful Asset*

Time matters more than talent.

Two players with identical skills will end up in very different places if one starts earlier and stays consistent.

The same is true with investing. Starting early gives compounding room to work. Waiting forces you to take more risk later to catch up.

In hockey terms, this is like skipping training camp and hoping to be ready for the playoffs.

You cannot compress preparation. You cannot rush compounding. The work has to happen over time.

## *The Real Cost of Waiting*

Waiting feels harmless.

"I'll start when I make more."

"I'll start after this season."

"I'll start when things settle down."

Those delays have a cost. Not just financially, but psychologically. Habits get harder to build. Discipline erodes. Momentum disappears.

In hockey terms, this is drifting during the season instead of addressing issues early. Small problems become big ones.

Waiting forces future you to play catch-up. Catch-up usually requires taking risks you would not otherwise need.

## *Risk Should Be Managed, Not Eliminated*

Eliminating risk entirely means eliminating growth.

Managing risk means diversifying, staying disciplined, matching strategy to timeline, and avoiding emotional decisions.

In hockey terms, this is team defense. Everyone knows their role. Mistakes happen, but systems prevent them from becoming disasters.

Investing success is not about avoiding downturns. It is about surviving them without blowing up the plan.

## *Coach's Perspective*

A coach would not overcomplicate this.

- "Know your role."

- "Don't force it."
- "Stay within the system."
- "Next shift."
- "Trust the work."

Risk taken with preparation is confidence. Risk taken without structure is recklessness.

## *Game Situations and Decision Points*

**Situation 1:**

Markets drop sharply and headlines turn negative.

Do you panic, or do you recognize volatility as part of the game?

**Situation 2:**

You are behind where you want to be financially.

Do you chase high-risk plays, or do you recommit to disciplined consistency?

**Situation 3:**

You feel pressure to "make something happen."

Do you force a play, or trust compounding to do its job?

Every one of these moments tests patience more than intelligence.

## *Common Hockey Mistakes and Financial Parallels*

- **Forcing offense when tired**
- Financially: chasing returns late
- **Overreacting to momentum swings**
- Financially: selling during volatility
- **Ignoring development**
- Financially: waiting too long to start

The patterns repeat. Only the setting changes.

## *Winning the Long Game*

Risk is part of the game. Always has been.

The goal is not to avoid it, but to understand it, respect it, and use it wisely. Compounding rewards players who stay on the ice, shift after shift, season after season.

You do not need perfect timing. You need discipline and time.

That combination wins far more games than any single play ever will.

## *Athlete Takeaways*

- Risk creates opportunity when managed correctly
- Volatility is noise, not failure
- Compounding rewards consistency, not intensity
- Waiting costs more than people realize
- Stay disciplined and let time do the heavy lifting

# Chapter 11: Stocks Without the Highlight Reel

Every hockey player knows the difference between a smart play and a highlight play.

The highlight gets the crowd on its feet.

The smart play keeps you on the ice.

A no-look pass through traffic looks great when it works. Most of the time, it ends up going the other way. Coaches don't build winning teams around highlight reels. They build them around players who make the right play over and over again.

Stocks work the same way.

Most people think stock investing is about finding the next superstar. The hot company. The explosive move. The overnight success. That mindset creates excitement, but it rarely creates lasting results.

This chapter is about understanding what owning stock actually means, why growth and value both matter, how dividends quietly do work most people ignore, and why the biggest stock market myths hurt athletes more than they help.

## *What Owning Stock Actually Means*

When you buy a stock, you are not buying a ticker symbol.

You are buying ownership.

That ownership represents a claim on a real business. A company with employees, customers, products, cash flow, debt, competition, and management decisions. When the company grows profits over time, owners benefit. When it struggles, owners feel it.

In hockey terms, buying stock is like being invested in the organization, not just the top scorer. You are tied to the system, not just one shift.

Many athletes treat stocks like trading cards. Buy low, sell high, flip quickly. That approach ignores the core purpose of ownership.

Long-term stock investing is about participating in the growth of businesses over time. The stock price moves daily, but the underlying value changes much more slowly.

When you understand that, short-term noise becomes easier to ignore.

### *Why Stocks Feel Risky to Athletes*

Athletes are conditioned to react instantly.

You see the puck. You move. You get feedback immediately. Markets do not work that way.

Stock prices move constantly, but meaningfully understanding those moves takes time. That mismatch creates anxiety.

In hockey terms, this is like watching the scoreboard after every shift instead of trusting the game plan.

Stocks are volatile. That does not make them reckless. It makes them alive. Ownership means accepting fluctuation in exchange for growth.

The risk is not movement. The risk is abandoning the plan.

### *Growth vs Value Investing*

Growth and value are two different ways to approach ownership.

**Growth investing** focuses on companies expected to expand faster than average. These companies often reinvest profits, innovate aggressively, and trade at higher prices relative to current earnings.

**Value investing** focuses on companies that appear undervalued based on fundamentals. They may be boring. Established. Less exciting. Often ignored.

In hockey terms, growth investing is playing an up-tempo, high-skill game. More upside, more volatility. Value investing is playing structured, defensive hockey. Less flash, more control.

Neither approach is inherently better. Both require discipline. Both can work in the right system.

Problems arise when athletes chase growth without understanding risk, or dismiss value because it lacks excitement.

Winning teams need skill players and grinders. Winning portfolios need growth and stability.

## *Dividends and the Importance of Total Return*

Dividends are often misunderstood or ignored.

A dividend is a portion of profits paid directly to shareholders. Some companies prioritize steady income. Others focus entirely on reinvestment.

In hockey terms, dividends are depth scoring. They don't dominate highlights, but they win games.

Total return includes both price appreciation and income. Focusing only on price movement misses half the picture.

Athletes often chase stock prices the same way they chase stats. Points matter, but so does defensive play, ice time, and consistency.

Dividends create cash flow, reduce reliance on selling shares, and add stability to long-term strategies. Over time, reinvested dividends can meaningfully compound results.

Ignoring them because they are "boring" is like ignoring faceoffs because they don't show up on SportsCenter.

## *Why Stock Picking Feels Tempting*

Stock picking feels competitive.

You beat the market. You found something early. You outsmarted everyone else. That narrative appeals to athletes.

The problem is that professional investors with massive resources struggle to consistently beat the market. Information is widely available. Prices reflect expectations quickly.

In hockey terms, this is trying to beat elite goalies by shooting from bad angles because it worked once.

Occasional wins happen. Sustained success is rare.

This does not mean stock picking is impossible. It means it should not be the foundation of a financial plan.

Ownership works best when paired with diversification, patience, and humility.

## *Common Stock Market Myths*

**Myth 1: Stocks are gambling**

Gambling is relying on chance without a system. Investing in businesses over time with discipline is not gambling.

**Myth 2: You need to time the market**

Timing feels powerful. It is incredibly difficult. Long-term participation matters more than perfect entry points.

**Myth 3: You need to find the next big thing**

You do not need one massive winner. You need consistent exposure to growth.

**Myth 4: Volatility means danger**

Volatility is movement. Danger comes from panic and poor decisions.

**Myth 5: More activity means better results**

Overtrading often reduces returns. Just like overplaying top lines leads to fatigue.

## *Stocks as Part of a System*

Stocks are not meant to stand alone.

They work best when combined with bonds, cash, diversification, and a clear time horizon. The goal is not maximum excitement. The goal is sustainability.

In hockey terms, this is line balance. You don't stack one line and ignore the rest of the roster.

Ownership should fit into a broader strategy, not dominate it emotionally.

## *Coach's Perspective*

A coach would keep it simple.

- "Make the smart play."
- "Don't force offense."
- "Stay within the system."
- "Trust the process."
- "One shift at a time."

Highlight plays come and go. Championships come from consistency.

## *Game Situations and Decision Points*

**Situation 1:**

A stock you own drops sharply.

Do you panic, or review whether the business changed?

**Situation 2:**

A friend brags about a hot stock.

Do you chase it, or stick to your plan?

**Situation 3:**

Markets feel boring.

Do you overtrade to feel active, or stay disciplined?

These moments define outcomes.

*Common Hockey Mistakes and Financial Parallels*

- **Trying to score on every shift**
- Financially: overtrading
- **Ignoring defensive responsibilities**
- Financially: ignoring diversification
- **Playing for the crowd**
- Financially: chasing hype

The patterns are familiar.

*Winning the Long Game*

Stocks reward patience, ownership, and discipline.

They punish impatience, ego, and reaction. You do not need to be perfect. You need to stay invested, diversified, and committed.

The goal is not to win the highlight reel. The goal is to stay in the lineup for decades.

That is how real wealth is built.

*Athlete Takeaways*

- Owning stock means owning a business, not chasing a ticker
- Growth and value both have roles on the roster
- Dividends quietly contribute to winning seasons
- Stock myths hurt discipline more than markets do
- Smart, boring consistency beats highlight-reel investing

# Chapter 12: Bonds and Playing Responsible Defense

Every championship hockey team understands one truth.

You can have elite scorers, explosive speed, and highlight-reel goals, but if you do not play responsible defense, the season ends early.

Defense does not get the crowd roaring every night. It does not dominate social media clips. But it keeps games winnable, protects leads, and creates stability when momentum swings.

Bonds play that exact role in a financial plan.

They are not flashy. They do not deliver massive short-term gains. What they do provide is structure, balance, and reliability. Bonds absorb pressure when markets get chaotic and help prevent one bad stretch from wrecking the entire season.

This chapter explains how bonds actually work, the risks involved, when they make sense, and why they are critical to a diversified portfolio, especially for athletes who understand the importance of staying disciplined over a long season.

## *Opening Shift: Defense Wins When Offense Struggles*

Every player remembers nights when goals were hard to come by.

The puck would not bounce right. Shots hit posts. Power plays stalled. Those are the games where disciplined defense keeps you alive. Blocking shots. Clearing the zone. Winning battles along the boards. Staying patient until the opportunity comes.

Bonds exist for those moments in your financial life.

Markets do not move in straight lines. Stocks have losing seasons. Sometimes multiple in a row. Bonds are built to absorb those stretches so you do not abandon the game plan.

## *How Bonds Work*

At their core, bonds are loans.

When you buy a bond, you are lending money to a borrower. That borrower could be a government, a municipality, or a corporation. In exchange, the borrower agrees to pay interest and return your principal at maturity.

In hockey terms, bonds are like structured systems. Everyone knows their role. The expectations are clear. The outcome is predictable if nothing breaks down.

Key components of a bond include:

- **Principal:** The amount you lend
- **Interest rate:** The payment you receive for lending
- **Maturity:** When the loan is repaid

Unlike stocks, bonds do not represent ownership. They represent obligation. That difference matters when markets get stressed.

## *Why Bonds Behave Differently Than Stocks*

Stocks fluctuate based on growth expectations, profits, and emotion. Bonds fluctuate based on interest rates, credit quality, and time.

That difference creates diversification.

When stocks struggle, bonds often provide stability. Not always, but often enough to matter. This is why bonds are rarely about maximizing returns.

They are about managing risk.

In hockey terms, bonds are defensive positioning. You are not trying to score from your own zone. You are preventing odd-man rushes and limiting damage.

## *Interest Rate Risk Explained*

Interest rate risk is one of the most misunderstood bond risks.

When interest rates rise, existing bonds with lower rates become less attractive, and their prices fall. When rates fall, existing bonds become more valuable.

This does not mean bonds are broken when rates rise. It means prices fluctuate.

For long-term investors who hold bonds to maturity, interest rate movement matters less than cash flow and principal return.

In hockey terms, this is like line matching. Certain matchups are uncomfortable, but the system still works if you stay disciplined.

Short-term movement is not failure. Panic is.

## *Credit Risk and Defensive Awareness*

Credit risk refers to the borrower's ability to repay the loan.

Government bonds typically carry lower credit risk. Corporate bonds vary widely. Higher interest rates often mean higher risk.

This mirrors defensive assignments. Some matchups are safer. Others require more awareness and support.

Chasing high-yield bonds without understanding credit risk is like pinching aggressively with no coverage behind you. It works until it doesn't.

Responsible defense means knowing who you are matched against and adjusting accordingly.

### *When Bonds Make Sense*

Bonds are not an all-or-nothing decision.

They make sense in different amounts depending on:

- Time horizon
- Income stability
- Risk tolerance
- Career stage

For younger athletes with long timelines, bonds may play a smaller role. For athletes transitioning careers, protecting capital becomes more important.

In hockey terms, rookies play with energy. Veterans play with awareness.

Neither approach is wrong. They just reflect different responsibilities.

### *Bonds as Shock Absorbers*

One of the biggest values of bonds is psychological.

They reduce volatility. They smooth returns. They give investors confidence to stay invested when stocks struggle.

This matters more than spreadsheets suggest.

Athletes are competitive. Losses hurt. Seeing portfolios swing wildly creates emotional pressure that leads to bad decisions.

Bonds reduce that pressure.

They allow you to stay in the game instead of bailing during a slump.

### *The Role of Bonds in a Diversified Portfolio*

Diversification is not about maximizing returns in good years. It is about surviving bad ones.

Bonds help portfolios:

- Reduce volatility

- Provide income
- Preserve capital
- Create flexibility

They do not replace stocks. They complement them.

In hockey terms, you do not play all offense or all defense. You roll lines. You manage shifts. You protect leads intelligently.

A diversified portfolio does the same thing.

## *Coach's Perspective*

A coach would not overcomplicate this.

- "Defense first."
- "Stay in position."
- "Limit mistakes."
- "Protect the middle."
- "Win ugly if you have to."

Bonds represent discipline. They keep you from getting reckless when the game tightens.

## *Game Situations and Decision Points*

**Situation 1:**

Markets drop sharply.

Do you panic and sell stocks, or rely on your defensive structure?

**Situation 2:**

Interest rates rise and bond prices dip.

Do you abandon bonds, or remember their role?

**Situation 3:**

Someone tells you bonds are "dead."

Do you follow noise, or stick to fundamentals?

Defense rarely looks impressive until it is missing.

### *Common Hockey Mistakes and Financial Parallels*

- **Pinching at the wrong time**
- Financially: chasing yield without understanding risk
- **Ignoring defensive assignments**
- Financially: holding only aggressive investments
- **Panicking after one bad shift**
- Financially: reacting to short-term rate moves

These mistakes compound damage quickly.

### *Winning the Long Game*

Bonds are not designed to win scoring titles.

They are designed to help you finish seasons strong.

They protect against blowups, stabilize outcomes, and give you the confidence to stay invested through volatility. They turn chaos into structure.

The teams that win championships respect defense. The investors who build lasting wealth respect bonds.

You do not need them to shine. You need them to work.

### *Athlete Takeaways*

- Bonds are defense, not offense
- Interest rate movement is normal, not failure
- Credit risk requires awareness, not fear
- Bonds stabilize portfolios when pressure rises
- Responsible defense keeps you in the game long term

# Chapter 13: Funds, ETFs, and Line-Based Investing

No hockey team wins by rolling one guy for sixty minutes.

Championship teams win because they trust their lines. Different skill sets. Different roles. Different matchups. Everyone does their job, shift after shift, without trying to be the hero.

That is exactly how funds and ETFs work in investing.

Instead of trying to pick individual stocks and win every shift yourself, you build lines. You let groups of players work together. You trust systems over highlights. And you focus on consistency instead of chasing one perfect play.

This chapter breaks down mutual funds and ETFs, index versus active strategies, the quiet danger of fees, and how diversification can be simple instead of overwhelming.

## *Opening Shift: Why Lines Matter More Than Superstars*

Every player has seen it. A team with one elite scorer but no depth. When that player gets shut down, the entire offense disappears.

Coaches know better.

They roll four lines. They balance ice time. They trust systems. Over the course of a long season, depth wins more games than raw star power.

Financially, funds and ETFs exist for the same reason. They give you depth. They spread risk. They allow you to participate in growth without needing to outsmart everyone else.

## *What Mutual Funds and ETFs Actually Are*

At a basic level, both mutual funds and ETFs pool money from many investors and invest it across multiple securities.

Think of them as full lines instead of individual players.

Instead of buying one stock, you buy exposure to dozens, hundreds, or even thousands of companies at once.

That immediately reduces risk.

The difference is not what they own. The difference is how they are structured and traded.

## *Mutual Funds Explained*

Mutual funds are traditional pooled investments.

You buy and sell them at the end of the trading day at the fund's net asset value. The manager decides what to buy and sell inside the fund.

From a hockey perspective, this is like a structured system run entirely by the coaching staff. Players execute what is called from the bench.

Pros of mutual funds:

- Professional management
- Automatic reinvestment
- Simplicity for long-term investors

Cons:

- Often higher fees
- Less control over timing
- Sometimes tax inefficient

Mutual funds are not bad. They just require trust in the system and awareness of costs.

### *ETFs Explained*

ETFs, or exchange-traded funds, trade like stocks.

You can buy or sell them during the day. They often track indexes and usually have lower fees.

In hockey terms, ETFs are like lines that are clearly defined, transparent, and easy to deploy. You know who is on the ice. You know their role.

Pros of ETFs:

- Lower fees
- Tax efficiency
- Flexibility

Cons:

- Easier to overtrade
- Temptation to time the market

ETFs reward discipline. Used correctly, they are powerful tools. Used emotionally, they become distractions.

### *Index Investing: Playing the System*

Index funds simply track a market index. No guessing. No predicting. No heroics.

This is like playing within a proven system. You trust structure over improvisation. You accept that some nights will be quiet, but the system wins over time.

Index investing:

- Embraces market returns

- Minimizes costs
- Reduces mistakes

It is not exciting. It is effective.

Most professional athletes understand this instinctively. You do not abandon the system because of one bad period.

## *Active Investing: Line Matching and Risk*

Active funds attempt to outperform the market.

Sometimes they succeed. Often they do not. And higher fees make the bar even harder to clear.

Active investing is like aggressive line matching. It can work with the right coach, the right personnel, and the right execution. But it increases risk.

The question is not whether active investing can work. The question is whether it consistently works net of fees.

Most evidence says it is harder than advertised.

## *Fees: The Silent Momentum Killer*

Fees are one of the most important topics investors ignore.

A one percent fee sounds small. Over time, it is enormous.

Fees quietly reduce returns every year, regardless of performance. They compound in reverse.

In hockey terms, fees are like poor line changes. Nobody notices at first. Over a season, they cost goals.

The lower your fees, the more of your effort stays on the scoreboard.

This is why index funds and ETFs are so powerful. They minimize unnecessary drag.

### *Expense Ratios and Why They Matter*

Every fund has an expense ratio.

That is the annual cost of running the fund. It comes out whether markets go up or down.

Lower expense ratios:

- Improve long-term outcomes
- Increase consistency
- Reduce pressure to chase returns

You cannot control markets. You can control costs.

That is a coach's mentality.

### *Diversification Without Complexity*

Many investors think diversification requires complexity.

It does not.

A handful of well-chosen funds can provide exposure across:

- Stocks
- Bonds
- Domestic markets
- International markets

This is like building balanced lines instead of overloading one unit.

More funds do not automatically mean more diversification. Sometimes they mean overlap, confusion, and poor execution.

Simple systems are easier to stick with.

### *Coach's Perspective*

A coach would keep this message short:

- "Roll your lines."
- "Trust the system."
- "Do not freelance."
- "Details matter."
- "Stop trying to win the game in one shift."

Funds and ETFs reward patience and discipline. They punish impatience and ego.

### *Game Situations and Decision Points*

**Situation 1:**
You hear about a hot stock everyone is buying.
Do you chase it, or trust your lineup?
**Situation 2:**
Markets drop and your ETF is down.
Do you panic, or stay in structure?
**Situation 3:**
Someone pitches a complex strategy with high fees.
Do you buy the hype, or stick to fundamentals?
Winning investors respond the same way winning teams do.
They stay composed.

### *Common Hockey Mistakes and Financial Parallels*

- **Shortening the bench too early**
- Financially: abandoning diversification
- **Trying to score every shift**
- Financially: stock picking without a plan

- **Ignoring conditioning**
- Financially: ignoring fees
- **Overcoaching**
- Financially: too many funds, too many changes

Systems fail when discipline breaks down.

## *Winning the Long Game*

Funds and ETFs are not shortcuts.

They are infrastructure.

They allow you to stay invested, reduce mistakes, and participate in growth without needing to predict the future.

Over decades, that consistency compounds into meaningful wealth.

Hockey championships are built on depth, trust, and repetition. Wealth is built the same way.

You do not need to be flashy. You need to be reliable.

## *Athlete Takeaways*

- Funds and ETFs are lines, not individual stars
- Index strategies reward discipline and patience
- Fees quietly erode performance over time
- Diversification works best when it stays simple
- Trust the system and roll your lines consistently

# Chapter 14: Real Estate and Alternative Plays

In hockey, not every scoring chance comes from the same look.

Some goals come off clean breakaways. Others come from rebounds, deflections, or grinding along the boards until space opens up. Smart teams understand that offense is not one-dimensional. You take what the game gives you, but you never abandon structure.

Real estate and alternative investments work the same way.

They are not the first plays you learn in training camp, and they are not required to win early in your career. But over time, they can become valuable complementary pieces if you understand their role, risks, and limitations.

This chapter is about knowing when these plays make sense, when they do not, and how to avoid getting caught out of position.

## *Opening Shift: Big Ice, Heavy Legs*

Every player remembers the first time they moved up a level and the ice suddenly felt bigger.

The game slowed down in some ways and sped up in others. You had more space, but mistakes were punished harder. You could not rely on raw effort alone anymore. You had to think ahead.

That is what happens when investors start considering real estate and alternatives.

The opportunity feels bigger. The numbers feel larger. The conversations sound more sophisticated. But the margin for error also gets thinner.

If you jump in without understanding positioning, you can get burned fast.

### *Renting vs Owning: Ice Time Flexibility*

The first real estate decision most athletes face is renting versus owning.

Renting is flexibility. You pay for shelter and move on. No long-term commitment. No surprise repairs. No tying up capital.

In hockey terms, renting is like being a call-up. You are mobile. You can change teams, leagues, or cities without being anchored.

Owning is commitment. You build equity over time, but you take on responsibility. Maintenance, taxes, insurance, and market risk all come with the territory.

Owning is like signing a longer contract. It can be rewarding, but only if it fits your stage of life and your role.

Financially, owning only makes sense when:

- You plan to stay put long enough
- Your income is stable
- You have cash reserves
- You are comfortable with illiquidity

Buying a home too early can limit flexibility and create pressure when life changes.

### *Real Estate as an Investment*

Many athletes hear that real estate is "safe" or "always goes up."

That is a myth.

Real estate can be powerful, but it is not guaranteed. It is local, illiquid, and management-intensive.

Owning investment property is like playing heavy minutes. It can wear you down if you are not prepared.

Risks include:

- Vacancy
- Repairs
- Market downturns
- Financing risk
- Time and energy costs

Returns are often uneven. Some years are great. Others are frustrating.

Real estate rewards patience, capital, and systems. It punishes emotion and poor planning.

### *REITs: Playing the Same Game From the Bench*

REITs, or real estate investment trusts, allow you to invest in real estate without owning property directly.

You get exposure to real estate income and appreciation, but without fixing toilets or chasing tenants.

In hockey terms, REITs are like contributing from the second unit. You are involved, but you are not carrying the physical load.

Benefits of REITs:

- Liquidity
- Diversification
- Lower capital requirements
- Professional management

Trade-offs:

- Market volatility
- No direct control
- Income can fluctuate

REITs can be a smart way to add real estate exposure while maintaining flexibility.

## *Alternatives: Not Every Play Belongs in the Game Plan*

Alternatives include things like commodities, private equity, hedge funds, private credit, and collectibles.

These sound impressive. They are often pitched as exclusive or sophisticated.

But sophistication does not equal suitability.

In hockey terms, alternatives are specialty plays. They might work in specific situations, but they are not the foundation of your offense.

Key characteristics of alternatives:

- Less transparency
- Higher fees
- Limited liquidity
- Complex risks

Some alternatives make sense for experienced investors with excess capital. Many do not.

The danger is believing that complexity equals advantage.

## *Liquidity: Can You Get Off the Ice?*

Liquidity matters more than most athletes realize.

Liquidity is your ability to access money quickly without penalty or loss.

Stocks and ETFs are liquid. Real estate and alternatives often are not.

In hockey terms, liquidity is your line change. If you cannot get off the ice, fatigue sets in and mistakes happen.

Illiquid investments can create problems when:

- Income changes

- Emergencies arise
- Opportunities appear
- Life transitions happen

Before committing to illiquid investments, you need strong cash flow and reserves.

### *Risk Looks Different Off the Scoreboard*

Real estate and alternatives carry risks that do not show up daily.

Markets may not update every day, but that does not mean risk disappears. It just hides.

Lack of price movement does not mean stability. It often means delayed feedback.

This is like not seeing the scoreboard change but still getting outplayed.

Understanding true risk requires looking beyond surface calm.

### *Coach's Perspective*

A coach would say it plainly:

- "Earn the right to expand your game."
- "Do not get cute."
- "Know your role."
- "Position before opportunity."
- "If you do not understand it, do not play it."

Real estate and alternatives are optional tools, not requirements.

You win more games by avoiding bad mistakes than by chasing flashy opportunities.

## *Game Situations and Decision Points*

**Situation 1:**

You feel pressure to buy property because everyone else is doing it.

Do you follow the crowd, or wait until it fits your life?

**Situation 2:**

You are pitched a private investment with high minimums and limited access.

Do you trust the story, or demand clarity?

**Situation 3:**

You need cash unexpectedly, but your money is locked up.

Was liquidity properly planned?

Good decisions are made before pressure hits.

## *Common Hockey Mistakes and Financial Parallels*

- **Trying plays outside your skill set**
- Financially: investing in assets you do not understand
- **Overcommitting ice time**
- Financially: tying up too much capital
- **Ignoring conditioning**
- Financially: ignoring cash flow
- **Chasing highlight goals**
- Financially: chasing alternative investments

Structure protects you when conditions change.

## *Winning the Long Game*

Real estate and alternatives are not shortcuts.

They are complements.

For many athletes, the foundation remains boring and effective investments like diversified funds, consistent saving, and disciplined behavior.

Once that base is solid, selective real estate or alternatives can add value.
Just like hockey, timing matters. Role matters. Structure matters.
You do not win by playing every position at once.
You win by playing your position well, shift after shift.

### *Athlete Takeaways*

- Renting offers flexibility; owning requires stability
- Real estate demands time, capital, and patience
- REITs provide exposure without hands-on management
- Alternatives increase complexity and reduce liquidity
- Never sacrifice structure chasing a flashy play

# Part IV: Managing the Game and the Season

Championships are won through adjustments.

Every hockey season follows the same basic pattern. You come out of training camp with a plan. Lines are set. Roles are defined. Systems are installed. Everyone knows what the team is trying to do.

And then the season starts.

Injuries happen. Matchups change. Confidence swings. Hot streaks and cold streaks appear. What worked in October does not always work in February. The teams that survive are not the ones with the prettiest plan on paper. They are the ones that adjust without panicking.

Money works the same way.

You do not build a financial plan once and forget about it. You manage it across seasons, stages, and situations. This part of the book is about learning how to make smart adjustments while keeping your identity intact.

## *The Difference Between a Game Plan and Coaching*

In hockey, a game plan sets direction. Coaching manages reality.

You might want to play fast, aggressive, forechecking hockey. But if your lineup changes, if you are facing a different opponent, or if fatigue sets in, adjustments are required. The goal is not to abandon your style. The goal is to apply it correctly given the situation.

Financially, your long term plan is your system. Asset allocation, saving rate, and goals define who you are trying to be.

Managing the game means:

- Adjusting contributions
- Rebalancing risk
- Responding to life changes
- Ignoring noise while staying aware

The worst mistake is either overreacting or refusing to adjust at all.

### *Adjustments Are Not Panic Moves*

Good teams adjust calmly. Bad teams chase the puck.

In money, panic shows up when people:

- Make changes based on headlines
- Chase recent performance
- Abandon long term strategy after short term losses
- Overcorrect after one bad stretch

That is like blowing up line combinations after one bad shift.

Adjustments should be planned, measured, and purposeful. They should be made because conditions changed, not because emotions spiked.

### *Seasons Change, Roles Change*

In hockey, your role evolves.

A rookie plays limited minutes. A veteran manages energy. A leader understands when to push and when to steady the bench.

Your financial role changes too.

Early in your career, the focus is on:

- Building habits

- Establishing savings
- Learning discipline

Mid career shifts toward:

- Managing complexity
- Protecting what you have built
- Balancing growth with stability

Later stages emphasize:

- Preservation
- Income planning
- Risk reduction

Managing the season means understanding where you are and playing accordingly.

## *Momentum Is Real, But It Lies*

Every player believes in momentum. Confidence matters. Rhythm matters. But momentum can be misleading.

A hot streak can make you reckless. A cold stretch can make you desperate.

Financial markets create the same illusion. Strong returns make people believe they are smarter than they are. Down markets make people doubt systems that have worked for decades.

The job is not to chase momentum. The job is to stay disciplined when momentum tempts you to abandon fundamentals.

### *Adjusting Without Losing Identity*

Great teams do not change who they are every night. They adjust details, not identity.

Financially, this means:

- Rebalancing instead of rebuilding
- Tweaking contributions instead of abandoning plans
- Updating goals without rewriting everything

If your strategy requires constant reinvention, it was never strong to begin with.

### *Coach's Perspective*

A coach managing a long season would remind you:

Stick to the system.

Do not cheat the game.

Details matter.

One shift at a time.

Trust the process.

Adjustments are part of the plan, not evidence that the plan failed.

### *What This Section Will Teach You*

In the chapters that follow, you will learn how to:

- Position your portfolio correctly for your role
- Make buying and holding decisions with discipline
- Rebalance without overcoaching
- Handle emotional pressure and outside noise

These are not flashy skills. They are winning skills.

The difference between teams that fade and teams that finish strong is not talent. It is management.

## *Managing the Season Off the Ice*

Hockey players understand this instinctively. You do not sprint through an entire season. You pace yourself. You manage recovery. You adjust effort based on schedule, travel, and opponent.

Money is no different.

Trying to win every day financially leads to burnout and mistakes. Winning over time requires patience, discipline, and trust in preparation.

This part of the book focuses on staying upright through the grind.

Because championships are not won in highlight moments.

They are won in quiet adjustments, shift after shift, over a long season.

# Chapter 15: Asset Allocation and Line Combinations

**Every hockey player understands line combinations.**

You do not throw five scorers on the ice and hope it works. You balance skill sets. You mix speed with strength, offense with defense, experience with energy. A good line has chemistry. A great line has balance.

When coaches get line combinations right, the game slows down. Pucks move cleaner. Defensive gaps tighten. Offense becomes sustainable instead of frantic.

Asset allocation works the same way.

It is not about picking the single best investment. It is about putting the right pieces together so your financial lineup performs across different situations, opponents, and seasons.

## The Investing Concept Explained Through Hockey

Asset allocation is how you divide your money among stocks, bonds, and cash.

In hockey terms, this is how you build your lines.

Stocks are your scorers. They drive growth, create offense, and push the pace. They can change the game quickly, but they also take risks. Fast breaks lead to goals, but they can also lead to odd man rushes the other way.

Bonds are your defensive forwards and defensemen. They stabilize play, reduce volatility, and protect leads. They may not make highlight reels, but they keep the game under control when momentum shifts.

Cash is your bench and penalty kill unit. It provides flexibility, liquidity, and quick response when conditions change. It is not flashy, but when a penalty hits or an opportunity opens up, cash lets you respond immediately.

Financially, this works the same way as line combinations. Too much offense and you give up odd man rushes. Too much defense and you struggle to score. Too much sitting back and you lose momentum.

The goal is balance based on your role, your season, and your long-term plan.

## Stocks, Bonds, and Cash Balance

Many athletes make the mistake of overloading one line.

Early success in stocks can make people feel invincible. A few strong years in the market and it feels like you found the perfect line combination. But market downturns expose the lack of defensive structure fast.

On the other side, being overly conservative can limit growth and leave long-term goals underfunded. If you never send a scoring line over the boards, you might keep the game close, but you will struggle to win.

A well-built financial lineup recognizes that:

Stocks create long-term growth

Bonds reduce volatility and provide stability

Cash allows you to adapt and respond

You do not win a season with only one line. You win by rolling all four lines responsibly. You give different units ice time depending on the situation, but no single group carries everything alone.

## Domestic vs International Exposure

Hockey is global.

The NHL pulls talent from North America, Europe, and beyond. Different styles exist. Different leagues produce different strengths. Teams that scout broadly gain depth and resilience.

Investing internationally works the same way.

Domestic investments keep you tied to your home market. International exposure adds diversification by spreading risk across economies, currencies, and growth cycles.

Financially, this is like having players trained in different systems. Some regions perform well when others struggle. International exposure does not guarantee higher returns every year, but it reduces reliance on one country or one economic engine.

Ignoring global markets is like refusing to draft European players because you only trust what you know. You might survive, but you limit your ceiling and your resilience.

## Diversification Principles

Diversification is not about owning more stuff. It is about owning different stuff that behaves differently.

In hockey terms, diversification means:

Different player roles

Different skill sets

Different usage situations

If everyone on your team plays the same way, opponents adjust quickly. If your portfolio reacts the same way to every market event, risk compounds.

Diversification spreads responsibility across the lineup. When one unit struggles, another can carry the load. A checking line can hold the fort. A power play unit can break through. A strong goaltender can buy time.

That balance is what keeps you competitive across a long season, not just a hot streak.

## Career-Stage Allocation

Your role changes over time.

A rookie does not play the same minutes as a veteran. A veteran does not play the same style as a rookie. Coaches adjust usage based on age, experience, and durability.

Financial allocation must evolve with your career stage.

Early career: More growth oriented. You can take more risk because time is on your side. If a season is rough, you have years to recover.

Mid-career: Balance becomes critical. You are building while protecting progress. Responsibilities grow. Your lineup needs both offense and structure.

Later career: Stability and income matter more. Preserving leads matters as much as scoring goals. You are managing energy and minimizing big mistakes.

Ignoring career stage is like playing a 40-year-old veteran like a 19-year-old rookie. It looks aggressive until something breaks.

## Coach's Perspective

What would a coach say about asset allocation?

"Roll the lines."

"Play within your role."

"Balance wins championships."

"Do not chase every hit."

"Trust the lineup."

A coach would never judge a player on one shift. Likewise, your financial lineup should not be judged on one year.

Consistency beats intensity.

## Game Situations and Decision Points

**Situation 1:**

You experience a strong run in stocks and your portfolio becomes heavily tilted toward offense.

Do you rebalance or ride the hot hand?

Financial lesson: Winning teams rebalance. They protect leads instead of gambling them. Letting one line play the whole game looks exciting until fatigue and mistakes set in.

**Situation 2:**

Markets decline and bonds feel boring compared to past returns.

Do you cut defense to chase offense?

Financial lesson: Defense exists to protect you when offense struggles. You do not bench your best defensive players because they are not scoring.

**Situation 3:**

A new job or income increase changes your role.

Do you keep the same lineup or adjust responsibilities?

Financial lesson: Career changes require lineup adjustments, not panic trades. More income can allow more offense, but only if the rest of the structure stays intact.

## Common Athlete Mistakes and Financial Parallels

Athletes often:

Overvalue scoring and undervalue defense

Chase highlights instead of consistency

Believe talent alone will carry them

Financially, this leads to:

Overconcentration in risky assets

Ignoring diversification

Emotional decision-making

The same habits that hurt teams hurt portfolios.

## Winning the Long Game

Asset allocation is not about predicting the next opponent. It is about preparing for the entire season.

Well-built line combinations:

Survive injuries

Handle slumps

Adapt to different matchups

Well-built portfolios do the same.

Some athletes will experience sudden income or opportunity. That does not change the need for balance. In fact, it increases the need for discipline. The bigger the contract, the more important structure becomes.

Championship teams are not built on one superstar line. They are built on depth, structure, and chemistry.

## Athlete Takeaways

Build your portfolio like line combinations, not a shootout lineup

Balance offense, defense, and flexibility at all times

Adjust roles as your career changes

Diversification keeps you competitive when conditions shift

Championships are won by balanced teams, not highlight reels

# Chapter 16: Buying, Holding, and Staying Disciplined

Every hockey player remembers the first time they got benched for doing too much.

You jump on the ice feeling good. You try to force a play that is not there. You skate past your support. You take a low-percentage shot instead of cycling the puck. The play dies, momentum swings, and the coach gives you that look.

Hockey punishes impatience.

The best players are not the ones who make the flashiest move every shift. They are the ones who understand timing, trust the system, and stay disciplined even when the crowd wants more.

Investing works the same way.

Buying, holding, and staying disciplined is not exciting. It is effective. And over a full season, it wins far more games than chasing highlights.

## *Opening and Funding Accounts: Getting on the Ice the Right Way*

You cannot contribute if you are not on the ice.

In investing, opening accounts is simply getting yourself into the game. Brokerage accounts, retirement accounts, and savings vehicles are your locker room access. Without them, talent and intention do not matter.

Financially, this works the same way as getting dressed properly before warmups. Skates tied. Helmet on. Stick taped. No shortcuts.

Funding accounts is your ice time. An account with no money does nothing. Consistent contributions matter more than perfect timing. Many athletes delay because they think they need a large amount to start. They do not.

Small, consistent contributions beat sporadic big deposits every time.

Waiting to feel "ready" is like waiting for the perfect shift. You will sit on the bench while the game passes you by.

## *Market Orders vs Limit Orders: Knowing How to Enter the Play*

Every entry into the zone has options.

Sometimes you dump the puck in and chase. Sometimes you carry it in with control. The choice depends on the situation, the opponent, and your role.

Market orders are like dumping the puck in. You accept the current price and move forward immediately. It is simple and efficient, especially for long-term investors who are focused on participation rather than precision.

Limit orders are like controlled entries. You set a price and wait. This can work well in specific situations but also risks missing the play entirely if conditions change.

Financially, the mistake many athletes make is overthinking entries. They obsess over the perfect price instead of focusing on long-term positioning. Over time, missing the market entirely hurts more than a slightly imperfect entry.

Execution matters more than perfection.

## *Buy-and-Hold Discipline: Trusting the System*

Every team has a system.

Breakouts, forechecks, defensive coverage. The system only works if players stick to it under pressure. The moment someone freelances, gaps appear.

Buy-and-hold investing is the financial equivalent of trusting the system.

You build a portfolio aligned with your goals, risk tolerance, and timeline. You rebalance periodically. You do not abandon the plan every time the market shifts.

Financially, this works the same way as playing through slumps. Every player goes cold. Every team loses games. Abandoning the system mid-season creates chaos.

Markets move. Volatility is normal. Long-term success comes from staying invested, not from jumping in and out based on emotion.

### *Avoiding Emotional Decisions: Playing the Shift, Not the Crowd*

Hockey is emotional.

Crowds roar. Momentum swings. One bad bounce can change a game. The best players are not emotionless, but they are controlled.

Investing punishes emotional decisions.

Fear leads to selling at the worst time. Greed leads to buying at inflated prices. Overconfidence leads to abandoning fundamentals.

Financially, this is like chasing a hit out of position or forcing a pass through traffic. The intent may be aggressive, but the outcome is usually negative.

Discipline means:

- Sticking to your plan when others panic
- Staying patient when returns feel slow
- Ignoring noise that does not align with your goals

The market rewards composure, not emotion.

### *Coach's Perspective*

What would a coach say about buying and holding?

- "Play your shift."
- "Trust the system."

- “Do not try to win the game in one play.”
- “Stay inside the structure.”
- “Next shift.”

A coach would not allow a player to abandon the game plan after one mistake. Financially, the same rule applies.

Consistency beats heroics.

## *Game Situations and Decision Points*

**Situation 1:**

Markets drop sharply and headlines scream disaster.

Do you sell to protect yourself or stick to your plan?

Financial lesson: Selling in panic locks in losses. Staying disciplined allows recovery.

**Situation 2:**

A hot investment dominates social media and locker room conversations.

Do you chase it or stick with your allocation?

Financial lesson: Chasing trends often means arriving late and exiting early.

**Situation 3:**

You receive a bonus or unexpected income

Do you spend impulsively or deploy it intentionally?

Financial lesson: Windfalls require structure, not emotion.

## *Common Athlete Mistakes and Financial Parallels*

Athletes often:

- Try to do too much too quickly
- Chase momentum instead of fundamentals
- Confuse effort with effectiveness

Financially, this shows up as:

- Overtrading
- Timing the market
- Abandoning long-term plans

The same habits that get players benched hurt investors over time.

### *Discipline Over a Full Season*

A hockey season is long.

There are hot streaks and cold streaks. Injuries. Travel. Back-to-backs. The teams that succeed are not the ones who dominate every night. They are the ones who show up consistently and play the same way regardless of circumstances.

Financial success is built the same way.

Buying, holding, and staying disciplined allows compounding to work. It allows volatility to smooth out. It allows goals to be funded over time instead of gambled on.

Some athletes experience sudden income or opportunity. That does not eliminate the need for discipline. It increases it. The more resources you have, the more costly emotional mistakes become.

### *Winning the Long Game*

Discipline is not passive. It is active restraint.

It is choosing not to react when others do. It is trusting preparation when pressure rises. It is staying inside your lane while others drift.

In hockey, discipline keeps you on the ice late in games.

In investing, discipline keeps you in the game long enough to win.

## *Athlete Takeaways*

- Get on the ice early and stay in the game
- Execute entries without obsessing over perfection
- Trust the system through slumps and noise
- Emotion costs shifts, games, and portfolios
- Championships are won by disciplined teams, not emotional ones

# Chapter 17: Rebalancing and Mid-Season Adjustments

**Every hockey season reaches a point where what worked in October does not work in February.**

Lines that clicked early lose chemistry. Injuries force changes. A rookie hits a wall. A veteran slows down. The standings tighten, and weaknesses get exposed.

Good coaches do not panic. They also do not pretend nothing has changed.

They review film. They adjust lines. They redistribute minutes. They rebalance responsibilities. The system stays intact, but the details evolve.

Investing works the same way.

Rebalancing is not about reacting to every shift in momentum. It is about making smart, intentional adjustments so your financial game plan stays aligned as conditions change.

## How Often to Review Investments: Watching the Film, Not Staring at the Scoreboard

Teams do not overhaul their system after every game. But they do watch film regularly.

Financially, reviewing investments is film study. It is checking alignment, not obsessing over daily results. Most long-term investors only need to review portfolios one or two times per year, with additional check-ins when life changes.

Reviewing too often creates noise. Not reviewing at all creates drift.

Think about staring at the scoreboard every shift. Your emotions would swing with every shot attempt. That is not how coaches evaluate performance. They look at structure, positioning, effort, and trends over time.

Your portfolio is the same. A single month or quarter rarely means much. But gradual drift in allocation, risk exposure, or contribution habits can quietly change your long-term outcome.

If a winger starts cheating defensively, it may not show up in one shift. Over time, it becomes a liability. Periodic reviews help you catch issues early without overreacting.

Key principle: Review with purpose, not emotion.

## What Rebalancing Actually Means

Rebalancing is the process of bringing your portfolio back to its intended mix after markets move.

Over time, certain investments grow faster than others. Stocks may outperform bonds. One region or sector may dominate. Without adjustments, your risk profile slowly changes, often without you noticing.

In hockey terms, this is like one line playing too many minutes because they are scoring. Eventually, fatigue sets in. Defensive coverage slips. The rest of the lineup loses rhythm.

Financially, rebalancing is redistributing ice time. You are not benching your best players. You are protecting the team over the full season.

Rebalancing forces you to:

Trim what has grown too large

Add to what has fallen behind

Restore balance without emotion

This feels uncomfortable because it runs against instinct. You are selling what has done well and buying what has lagged. But that discipline is exactly why it works.

It is one of the few systematic ways to buy low and sell high without trying to predict the future.

## Rebalancing Strategies: Small Adjustments, Not System Changes

Good coaches adjust lines. Bad coaches change systems mid-game.

There are several ways to rebalance, and none require dramatic action.

Some investors rebalance on a calendar, such as once per year. Others rebalance when allocations drift beyond a set range. Both approaches work when applied consistently.

Financially, this is like second-period adjustments. You are not rewriting the playbook. You are tightening gaps, cleaning up coverage, and improving execution.

The biggest mistake athletes make is thinking rebalancing means starting over. It does not.

Rebalancing is maintenance. Not reconstruction.

You are not questioning your entire strategy. You are preserving it.

## Life Changes and Portfolio Updates: When the Game Actually Changes

Sometimes adjustments are forced.

In hockey, injuries change everything. So do trades, promotions, or role changes. Coaches respond because the game environment has changed, not because of one bad shift.

Financially, major life events require updates:

Job changes

Income increases or decreases

Marriage or divorce

Children

Health changes

Approaching retirement

These are not market events. They are personal events. And they matter more than market noise.

Your time horizon, risk tolerance, and financial responsibilities evolve. Ignoring these changes is like playing the wrong position all season.

A single person in their 20s plays a different financial role than a parent in their 40s. A stable career phase requires a different approach than a transition period.

Rebalancing tied to life changes is strategic, not emotional. It keeps your system aligned with your real-world situation.

## Avoiding Over-Coaching: When Adjustments Hurt More Than Help

Every team has seen it.

A coach overreacts. Lines change every shift. Players stop trusting the system. Confidence erodes. Chaos replaces structure.

In investing, over-coaching shows up as:

Constant tinkering

Chasing performance

Selling after losses

Buying after runs

Financially, this is the equivalent of line juggling every period. No chemistry develops. No plan sticks.

The market already provides enough movement. You do not need to add more.

Activity feels productive. Discipline is often quiet.

Knowing when not to act is as important as knowing when to adjust.

Sometimes the best adjustment is none at all.

## Coach's Perspective

What would a good coach say about rebalancing?

"Stick to the system."

"Make smart adjustments, not emotional ones."

"Trust your preparation."

"Do not over-coach."

"The season is long."

A coach understands that structure creates freedom. The same is true financially. When your system is clear, you can make small changes without losing identity.

## Game Situations and Decision Points

**Situation 1:**

Your stock investments have grown much faster than bonds.

Do you let it ride or rebalance?

Financial lesson: Growth without balance increases risk quietly. What feels like momentum can turn into overexposure.

**Situation 2:**

Markets drop and your allocation shifts sharply.

Do you sell to feel better or rebalance to stay aligned?

Financial lesson: Rebalancing during downturns restores discipline and keeps fear from dictating decisions.

**Situation 3:**

You change jobs and your income increases significantly.

Do you keep the same plan or update it?

Financial lesson: Life changes matter more than market headlines. Your plan should evolve with your role.

## Common Athlete Mistakes and Financial Parallels

Athletes often:

Overreact to short-term performance

Lose trust in systems during slumps

Mistake activity for effectiveness

Financially, this becomes:

Overtrading

Market timing

Emotional decision-making

Rebalancing exists to protect you from yourself.

## Discipline Across the Full Season

Rebalancing is boring. That is why it works.

It requires humility. It requires patience. It requires accepting that you cannot predict every bounce.

Hockey championships are not won by constant reinvention. They are won by teams that adjust intelligently while staying true to their identity.

Financial success follows the same pattern.

Some athletes experience sudden income, contracts, or opportunities. That does not eliminate the need for rebalancing. It increases it. Bigger portfolios magnify mistakes.

Structure becomes more important as the stakes rise.

## Winning the Long Game

Rebalancing is how you stay competitive late in the season.

It keeps risk aligned. It preserves endurance. It protects you from burnout and panic.

You do not need to win every shift. You need to finish strong.

In hockey, smart adjustments keep you playing meaningful games in April.

In money, smart rebalancing keeps you on track for decades.

## Athlete Takeaways

Watch film, not the scoreboard

Make small adjustments without changing the system

Update your plan when life changes, not when emotions spike

Over-coaching kills chemistry and portfolios

Championships are won by teams that adjust without panic

# Chapter 18: The Mental Game of Money

Every hockey player knows this moment.

The game tightens. The crowd gets louder. One mistake can swing everything. You feel the shift change coming, but adrenaline tells you to stay out. The puck takes a bad bounce. Suddenly momentum flips.

The teams that survive these moments are not always the fastest or most skilled. They are the most composed.

Money works the same way.

The biggest threats to long-term financial success are rarely technical. They are mental. Fear. Greed. Overconfidence. Noise. These forces show up at the worst possible times and push people to abandon solid plans.

This chapter is about learning to play the mental game of money the same way elite players manage pressure on the ice.

## *Fear, Greed, and Overconfidence: The Three Penalties That Kill Momentum*

Every hockey player understands penalties. You do not need to slash someone to hurt your team. A lazy hook at the wrong time can change the game.

Financially, fear, greed, and overconfidence are mental penalties.

**Fear** shows up during market drops. Headlines scream. Accounts fall. The instinct is to get off the ice and stop the bleeding. But selling during panic often locks in losses instead of preventing them.

This is like dumping the puck blindly every time pressure comes. You survive the moment but lose possession long term.

**Greed** shows up during hot streaks. One asset is scoring at will. Everyone is talking about it. The temptation is to chase, add more, and abandon balance.

This is the equivalent of trying to score from impossible angles because you feel unstoppable.

**Overconfidence** shows up after success. A few good decisions turn into belief that you can outsmart the system. Risk increases quietly. Discipline slips.

This is the player who stops backchecking because they think they are above it.

All three penalties come from emotion, not strategy.

## *Crowd Noise and Herd Behavior: When the Bench Gets Loud*

Hockey crowds influence games. Momentum shifts. Home ice matters. Players feel it.

Money has crowds too. Financial news, social media, group chats, and headlines create constant noise. Everyone has an opinion. Everyone sounds confident.

Herd behavior happens when people move together without thinking independently. Markets amplify this instinct. When prices rise, confidence grows. When prices fall, fear spreads.

Financially, this works the same way as chasing momentum after a big hit or a loud chant. Emotion replaces execution.

The problem is simple. By the time something feels obvious, it is usually late.

Elite players learn to tune out the crowd. They listen to coaches, systems, and preparation. Financially, you must do the same.

The market does not reward excitement. It rewards discipline.

### *Why Discipline Fails Under Pressure*

Athletes often assume discipline is permanent. It is not.

Discipline is easiest when things are calm. It is hardest when pressure spikes. Money creates delayed feedback, which makes discipline even harder.

In hockey, a bad shift shows up immediately. On the scoreboard. On film. In ice time.

In money, bad decisions can take years to show consequences. That delay makes emotional mistakes feel harmless in the moment.

Fear convinces you to protect short term. Greed convinces you to chase upside. Overconfidence convinces you that rules do not apply.

Without systems, discipline collapses under pressure.

### *Building Systems for Discipline: Playing Within the System*

Great teams rely on systems because systems hold when emotions do not.

Financial systems serve the same purpose. They remove decision-making during high-pressure moments.

Examples include:

- Automatic contributions
- Predetermined asset allocation
- Rebalancing rules
- Long-term investment plans

These systems work like line structure and defensive assignments. You do not think your way through every shift. You trust the system.

Financially, this works the same way as rolling four lines. Consistency beats heroics.

Systems are not about being rigid. They are about protecting you from emotional mistakes.

## *Staying Composed During Volatility: Playing Through Chaos*

Volatility is normal. In hockey, pucks bounce. Ice gets chewed up. Referees miss calls.

Markets behave the same way. Prices move daily. News changes hourly. Volatility feels uncomfortable, but it is not the enemy.

Permanent loss comes from panic. Not from movement.

In hockey terms, volatility is like traffic in front of the net. It is messy, chaotic, and uncomfortable. But abandoning position creates bigger problems.

Staying composed means:

- Accepting short-term discomfort
- Trusting preparation
- Avoiding emotional reactions
- Executing fundamentals

This is mental toughness applied to money.

## *Coach's Perspective*

What would a coach say during financial chaos?

- "Control what you can control."
- "Stay composed."
- "Trust the system."
- "One shift at a time."
- "Do not beat yourself."

A good coach knows panic spreads faster than confidence. Leaders slow things down. Systems stabilize behavior.

Financial discipline requires the same leadership from you.

## *Game Situations and Decision Points*

**Situation 1:**

Markets drop sharply and everyone is talking about it.
Do you sell to feel better or stick to the plan?
Financial lesson: Fear feels urgent. Discipline feels boring. Boring wins.

**Situation 2:**

One investment has skyrocketed and dominates your portfolio.
Do you chase more or rebalance?
Financial lesson: Greed breaks balance quietly.

**Situation 3:**

You have had several good financial years.
Do you increase risk because you feel confident?
Financial lesson: Overconfidence is often followed by exposure.

## *Common Athlete Mistakes and Financial Parallels*

Athletes often:

- Play emotionally after a bad call
- Chase momentum instead of structure
- Believe success means rules no longer apply

Financially, this becomes:

- Panic selling
- Performance chasing
- Excessive risk-taking

The mental game determines outcomes long before the scoreboard does.

## *Pressure Is a Privilege*

Pressure means you are in the game.

Markets move because money is being allocated, risk is being taken, and opportunity exists. Volatility is not a sign of failure. It is the cost of participation.

The athletes who succeed long term understand this. They do not flinch. They do not chase noise. They trust their preparation.

Some players experience sudden income, signing bonuses, or opportunities. That does not eliminate the mental game. It intensifies it. Bigger money increases emotional stakes.

Systems matter even more when numbers get larger.

## *Winning the Long Game*

The mental game of money is not about avoiding emotion. It is about managing it.

Fear, greed, and confidence never disappear. The goal is to prevent them from driving decisions.

Hockey seasons are not won in October. They are won by teams that stay composed through slumps, injuries, and pressure moments.

Financial success follows the same arc.

You do not need to predict the market. You need to stay mentally tough inside it.

## *Athlete Takeaways*

- Emotions are penalties if you let them drive decisions
- Crowd noise is loud, but systems are louder
- Discipline must be built before pressure hits
- Volatility is part of the game, panic is optional
- Championships are won by players who stay composed when it gets chaotic

# Part V: Life After the Rink

For years, your world revolved around the rink. Practice schedules. Travel days. Games on weekends. Coaches setting expectations. Teammates holding you accountable. The season had structure, rhythm, and purpose built into it. Even the off season had a plan.

Then, at some point, the rink gets quieter.

Maybe it happens suddenly. An injury. A cut. Graduation. A contract that never comes. Or maybe it fades slowly as priorities shift and life pulls you in new directions. Either way, life after hockey arrives whether you are ready or not.

This part of the book is about that transition. Not just financially, but structurally and mentally.

Because the hardest part of life after the rink is not losing competition. It is losing the system that supported everything else.

## *The Shift Nobody Prepares You For*

Hockey teaches discipline through structure. You do not decide when practice happens. You do not negotiate conditioning. You do not wonder whether film matters. It is built in. The environment carries you, even on days when motivation runs low.

After hockey, that structure disappears.

No coach sets your calendar. No one tracks your reps. No one forces recovery days or pushes you when effort fades. The accountability that once surrounded you becomes optional.

Financially, this is where many former players struggle.

Saving becomes inconsistent. Planning gets delayed. Big decisions get pushed down the road. Nothing breaks immediately, so it feels harmless. But drift is dangerous precisely because it is quiet.

Life after the rink requires internal discipline to replace external structure. That is a skill few athletes ever had to practice while they were playing.

## *Money Becomes a Long Game, Not a Season*

In hockey, seasons have clear endpoints. Training camp. Regular season. Playoffs. Off season. You can see the finish line. You can pace yourself toward it.

Money does not work that way.

There is no final buzzer for financial decisions. Income, expenses, taxes, investing, and planning continue whether you are paying attention or not. The decisions you make in your 20s and 30s echo for decades.

This is where former players often underestimate the shift.

They are used to short windows. Short shifts. Immediate feedback. Money operates on delayed feedback. Good habits feel boring now but powerful later. Bad habits feel harmless now but expensive later.

In hockey, a mistake often shows up on the scoreboard that night. Financially, mistakes often show up years later, when flexibility is gone and options feel limited.

Life after the rink demands patience that feels unfamiliar, but that patience is where long term stability is built.

## *Identity Without the Jersey*

One of the biggest challenges after hockey is identity.

For years, you were introduced as a player. That label carried status, community, and purpose. It shaped how you saw yourself and how others saw you. When it goes away, many former athletes feel unmoored.

This matters financially.

Identity drives behavior. If you are still chasing the version of yourself that existed in the locker room, decisions often lean toward appearance instead of alignment. Spending becomes a way to signal success. Risk becomes a substitute for competition. Busyness replaces purpose.

The most successful transitions happen when players separate who they are from what they used to do.

Hockey gave you tools. Discipline. Resilience. Team awareness. Work ethic. Coachability. The ability to handle pressure. Those traits still matter, even if the rink does not.

Your identity is not "hockey player." That was a chapter. Your identity is built from the traits that hockey helped sharpen.

## *Structure Is the New Skill*

The players who thrive after hockey are not the ones who miss it the least. They are the ones who rebuild structure intentionally.

They create routines. Financial check ins. Savings systems. Investment plans. Career goals. Health habits. They understand that freedom without structure leads to drift.

They replace:

- Coaches with calendars
- Practices with personal systems
- Film review with reflection and planning

Financial structure works the same way.

Automated savings replace forced discipline. Investment plans replace emotional decisions. Regular reviews replace reactive behavior. Clear goals replace vague intentions.

Structure is not restrictive. It is protective. It protects you from emotional decisions, from drift, and from the slow erosion that happens when no one is watching.

## *Relationships, Community, and New Locker Rooms*

The locker room is hard to replace, but isolation is not the answer.

Life after the rink requires new teams. Work teams. Professional groups. Mentors. Friends who understand the transition. People who challenge you, support you, and help you see blind spots.

Financial decisions improve when perspective exists. Isolation amplifies emotion. Community tempers it.

This does not mean living in the past. It means carrying forward what worked and adapting it to a new environment.

The players who struggle most are often the ones trying to recreate the exact feeling hockey gave them. The players who thrive build something new while honoring where they came from.

## *Why This Part of the Book Matters*

Everything in earlier sections focused on mechanics. Budgeting. Investing. Taxes. Protection.

This part focuses on sustainability.

You can have perfect financial knowledge and still struggle if structure, identity, and discipline collapse. Life after the rink tests these areas more than any spreadsheet ever will.

The goal is not to replace hockey. The goal is to build a life that works without it.

Money is not the point. It is a tool that supports stability, flexibility, and opportunity in this next chapter.

The rink taught you how to prepare, compete, and endure.

Life after the rink is where you apply those lessons over a much longer game. And just like hockey, the players who adjust, stay disciplined, build structure, and think long term give themselves the best chance to win.

# Chapter 19: Taxes and Where You Keep the Puck

**In hockey, possession matters.**

You can skate hard, win battles, and generate chances, but if you keep turning the puck over in bad areas of the ice, you will spend the entire shift defending. Smart teams know where to keep the puck, when to move it, and how to protect it depending on the situation.

Taxes work the same way.

You do not just need to earn money or invest it well. You need to be intentional about where that money lives. The same dollar can produce very different outcomes depending on how it is taxed, when it is taxed, or whether it is taxed at all.

Most athletes focus on how much they make or how their investments perform. Very few think about puck placement. That oversight quietly costs careers' worth of progress.

## Opening Shift: Protecting the Middle of the Ice

Every coach drills this into players early. Do not turn the puck over in the middle of the ice. Bad things happen there.

In money, taxes are the middle of the ice.

You can train hard, invest well, and build income, but if you ignore taxes, you give up ground without realizing it. Taxes are not something you avoid completely, but they are something you manage intentionally. The goal is not perfection. The goal is avoiding unforced errors.

Smart teams do not force plays through traffic. Smart earners do not force money through inefficient tax paths when better ones exist.

## Taxable vs Tax-Advantaged Accounts

Think of accounts as zones on the ice.

**Taxable accounts** are like open ice with no boards. Everything is exposed.

Brokerage accounts, savings accounts, and checking accounts fall here. Interest, dividends, and capital gains can create tax bills along the way. These accounts offer flexibility and access, which is important. But they provide little protection from ongoing taxation.

**Tax-advantaged accounts** are like playing within structure.

Retirement accounts such as 401(k)s, 403(b)s, traditional IRAs, and Roth IRAs provide rules in exchange for tax benefits. You give up some flexibility, but you gain efficiency and protection from yearly tax drag.

In hockey terms, taxable accounts are open ice. Tax-advantaged accounts are protected zones. You need both. You just need to know when to use each.

If all your money sits in open ice, every turnover gets punished.

## Tax Deferred vs Tax-Free Growth

Not all tax-advantaged accounts work the same way. This is where strategy deepens.

**Tax-deferred accounts** allow you to postpone taxes. Contributions may reduce your taxable income today, but withdrawals later are taxed as ordinary income.

This is like clearing the puck under pressure. You buy time. You escape the zone. But you still have to deal with it later in the shift.

**Tax-free accounts**, most commonly Roth accounts, flip the script. You pay taxes now, but qualified growth and withdrawals are tax free in the future.

This is like a clean breakout that leads to controlled entry. The hard part has already been handled.

Neither option is always better. The right mix depends on income level, career stage, tax brackets now versus later, and future flexibility. Smart players do not rely on only one breakout strategy. Smart earners use both tax-deferred and tax-free buckets to keep options open.

## Asset Location: Where You Keep the Puck

Asset location is one of the most overlooked strategies in personal finance.

It answers a simple question: Which investments belong in which accounts?

Some investments generate more taxable income. Others are more tax efficient. Placing everything randomly is like sending the wrong line out in every situation.

High-income or tax-inefficient investments can create larger tax bills if placed in taxable accounts. These often make more sense inside tax-advantaged accounts. More tax-efficient investments may be better suited for taxable accounts where their tax impact is lighter.

In hockey terms, this is knowing which players you trust on the penalty kill, which ones you send out on the power play, and which ones you double-shift late in the game.

You do not deploy every player in every situation.

That is asset location. It is about environment, not just talent.

## How Taxes Affect Every Decision

Taxes are not just an investment issue. They touch almost everything.

Raises and bonuses

Side income and business revenue

Contract changes

Real estate decisions

Retirement timing

Athletes often struggle here because income can be uneven. One big year followed by a quieter one. Performance bonuses. Endorsements. NIL deals. Business ventures. All of this creates fluctuating tax situations.

Complexity is not a failure. It is a signal that planning matters more.

Ignoring taxes does not keep things simple. It just hands control to circumstance instead of strategy.

## Common Tax Mistakes Players Make

Most tax mistakes are not aggressive. They are passive.

Not contributing to tax-advantaged accounts

Cashing out retirement accounts early

Ignoring capital gains when selling investments

Failing to plan for uneven income

Assuming withholding equals planning

Waiting too long to ask for help

These mistakes rarely cause immediate pain. They show up later, quietly reducing flexibility and increasing stress.

In hockey terms, this is taking lazy penalties early in the game. You do not feel it right away, but it changes momentum, ice time, and energy later.

## Coach's Perspective: What Would Your Coach Say?

A coach would be direct.

"Protect the puck."

"Know the situation."

"Do not beat yourself."

"Details win games."

"Smart hockey beats flashy hockey."

Taxes reward preparation and discipline, not avoidance. You do not need to become a tax expert. You need to be intentional about where money flows and how decisions affect future options.

## Game Situations and Decision Points

You get a raise.

Do you increase spending immediately, or adjust retirement contributions and tax strategy first?

You earn bonus income.

Do you set aside money for taxes and plan ahead, or hope it works out later?

You open an investment account.

Do you think about tax placement, or only performance?

Each of these moments is puck management. Poor placement leads to defensive scrambles. Smart placement leads to sustained possession.

## Winning the Long Game

Taxes are not about minimizing what you pay this year at all costs. They are about maximizing what you keep over a lifetime.

Good tax strategy compounds quietly. You rarely notice it shift to shift. But over a career, it is the difference between constantly defending and playing with control.

You cannot avoid taxes entirely. You can decide how intelligently you play around them.

Just like hockey, the players and teams that protect the puck give themselves the best chance to win.

## Athlete Takeaways

Protect the puck. Where your money lives matters as much as how it performs

Use the right zone for the right play. Taxable, tax-deferred, and tax-free all have roles

Do not give up goals on unforced errors. Most tax mistakes come from inattention

Match your lineup to the situation. Asset location is about strategy, not prediction

Smart, disciplined play over time beats chasing highlights every shift

# Chapter 20: Retirement Accounts and Financial Independence

In hockey, nobody thinks the game is won in the first period.

You manage shifts. You roll lines. You pace yourself for a long season. Teams that chase everything early burn out. Teams that understand timing, depth, and structure are the ones still standing late.

Retirement planning works the same way.

Financial independence is not about quitting work early or hitting some magic age. It is about **control**. Control over your time. Control over your choices. Control over whether you stay on the ice because you want to, not because you have to.

Retirement accounts are not exciting. They are not flashy. But they are the systems that quietly build control over decades.

## *Opening Shift: Playing the Long Season*

Every player learns this early. You cannot play a full season like it is a single shift.

You train in the offseason for games months away. You build conditioning for periods you have not played yet. You trust that preparation creates freedom later.

Retirement accounts are offseason training for your future self.

They exist to turn today's effort into tomorrow's options. Ignore them, and you are always skating uphill. Use them consistently, and the game slows down in your favor.

## *Employer Plans and Pensions*

For many players, employer retirement plans are the first real system they encounter.

401(k)s, 403(b)s, and similar plans allow you to invest directly from your paycheck. That automatic structure matters more than most people realize. It removes friction and replaces intention with execution.

Employer matches are not a bonus. They are compensation.

In hockey terms, an employer match is a power play you did not draw yourself. You do not decline it. You take advantage of it every time.

Pensions still exist in some careers. They provide guaranteed income later in life, often based on years of service. They reward longevity and consistency, not heroics.

The common mistake is ignoring these benefits because they feel far away. The reality is that every season you delay participation costs you future ice time.

## *Traditional and Roth IRAs*

IRAs give you flexibility beyond employer plans.

**Traditional IRAs** allow for tax-deferred growth. You may get a tax deduction today, but withdrawals later are taxed as income.

**Roth IRAs** flip the equation. You pay taxes now, but qualified growth and withdrawals later are tax free.

In hockey terms, this is choosing between different game plans based on the opponent and situation.

Sometimes you clear the puck and buy time. Sometimes you carry it with control and keep pressure off yourself later. Neither approach is always right. The best teams can do both.

Using a mix of traditional and Roth accounts creates balance. Balance creates options.

## *Contribution Rules: Knowing the Lines and Ice Time*

Retirement accounts come with rules.

Contribution limits.

Income limits.

Eligibility rules.

Penalties for early withdrawals.

These rules are not designed to punish you. They are designed to keep you playing the long game.

In hockey terms, this is line management. You cannot play one line for sixty minutes. Structure exists to protect performance.

Understanding the rules allows you to plan intelligently instead of reacting emotionally. Players who ignore the rules often find themselves taking unnecessary penalties later.

## *Withdrawal Rules: Timing Matters*

Saving is only half the game.

At some point, retirement planning becomes retirement income planning. That is when withdrawals, taxes, and timing take center ice.

Different accounts are taxed differently when money comes out. Required minimum distributions may apply. Early withdrawals can trigger penalties.

In hockey terms, this is late-game management.

You do not dump the puck blindly when protecting a lead. You control possession, manage matchups, and stay disciplined.

The goal is not to withdraw the most money as fast as possible. The goal is to make money last as long as you do.

## *What Financial Independence Really Means*

Financial independence is not a finish line.

It is the ability to choose.

Choose when to work.

Choose what to work on.

Choose when to step back.

Choose how to support family.

Choose how to live.

Retirement accounts create this flexibility slowly, quietly, and reliably. They reward players who think in seasons, not shifts.

Athletes often struggle here because they are used to visible progress. Retirement accounts grow in the background. You do not feel them working day to day.

But neither do you feel conditioning until the third period.

### *Common Retirement Mistakes Players Make*

Most mistakes are rooted in impatience.

Waiting too long to start.

Skipping employer matches.

Cashing out accounts early.

Concentrating everything in one account type.

Ignoring withdrawal planning.

Assuming future income will fix today's neglect.

These mistakes rarely cause immediate pain. They shorten careers later.

In hockey terms, this is cutting corners in training camp and hoping talent carries you. It rarely does.

### *Coach's Perspective: What Would Your Coach Say?*

A coach would be direct.

"Trust the process."

"Play your role."

"Win your shifts."

"Do not cheat the work."

"Be patient."

Retirement planning is not about brilliance. It is about discipline, consistency, and showing up every day even when nobody is watching.

That mindset should feel familiar.

### *Game Situations and Decision Points*

Your employer offers a match. Do you contribute enough to capture it?

You qualify for a Roth IRA. Do you fund it or delay?

You want flexibility later. Do you build it now or hope for it later?

Every one of these decisions is a shift you cannot replay.

### *Winning the Long Game*

Financial independence is built the same way great teams are built.

Depth.

Discipline.

Consistency.

Smart adjustments.

Patience.

Retirement accounts are not exciting. They are powerful.

Use them.

Respect the rules.

Let time do the heavy lifting.

You do not win championships with one shift. You win them by stacking smart shifts over an entire season.

### *Athlete Takeaways*

- Retirement accounts are offseason training for your future self
- Employer matches are power plays. Never waste them
- Traditional and Roth accounts create lineup flexibility later
- Rules exist to protect the long season, not restrict you
- Financial independence is control, not a finish line

# Chapter 26: Losing the Schedule and Rebuilding Structure

**One of the biggest shocks after hockey has nothing to do with speed, strength, or skill.**

**It is structural.**

For most of your playing life, your calendar was not yours.

Practice times. Lift sessions. Team meetings. Travel days. Film review. Recovery protocols. Someone else designed the rhythm of your day, your week, and your season. All you had to do was show up and execute.

Then the rink goes quiet.

No more mandatory skates. No coach setting lines. No strength staff tracking reps. No trainer asking how you slept. What used to be enforced discipline becomes optional discipline.

And that transition quietly derails more former players than any lack of motivation ever could.

## Opening Shift: When the Schedule Disappears

Every hockey player knows this feeling.

The season ends. Training camp is months away, or maybe your playing days are over entirely. For the first time in years, nobody is telling you where to be or when to be there.

At first, it feels like freedom.

You sleep in. You skip a workout. You eat what you want. You tell yourself you deserve a break.

Nothing catastrophic happens right away. You still feel fine. You are still in decent shape. You still have time.

That is what makes it dangerous.

Routines slip quietly. Conditioning fades slowly. Structure erodes before performance does.

Financial habits follow the exact same pattern.

When structure disappears, discipline has to come from somewhere else. If it does not, drift takes over.

## From Mandatory Workouts to Optional Discipline

In hockey, discipline is built into the environment.

Miss a workout and someone notices. Skip practice and you lose ice time. Show up out of shape and it shows immediately in drills and shifts. Structure forces consistency whether you feel motivated or not.

After sports, that enforcement is gone.

You can skip budgeting.

Delay saving.

Ignore retirement contributions.

Carry debt longer than planned.

Nothing happens immediately. There is no coach blowing a whistle. No scoreboard flashing consequences. That delay is the trap.

In hockey terms, this is open ice with no whistle. You can coast for a while. Eventually, though, it shows up on the scoreboard.

Optional discipline is harder than mandatory discipline because there are no consequences in the moment. The consequences show up years later.

## How Lack of Structure Quietly Breaks Financial Habits

Very few former players struggle financially because of one dramatic mistake.

Most struggle because of erosion.

Saving becomes inconsistent.

Bills get paid late.

Spending creeps up.

Planning gets postponed.

Long-term goals fade into the background.

There is no single collapse. Just slow, quiet drift.

Athletes are used to accountability systems that catch small mistakes early. When those systems disappear, many assume their discipline will carry over automatically. Sometimes it does. Often, it does not.

In hockey terms, this is a team that stops tracking shifts and minutes. No one notices the fatigue until the third period, when the legs are gone and the game slips away.

## Replacing Practice Schedules With Personal Systems

Structure does not disappear after hockey.

It has to be rebuilt.

That means replacing external enforcement with internal systems.

Automatic transfers into savings and investment accounts

Scheduled financial check-ins

Calendar reminders for bills and reviews

Rules that reduce emotional decision-making

In hockey terms, this is self-directed training.

Nobody is forcing you into the gym. You build your own plan. You commit to it. You follow it even when motivation drops.

The goal is not intensity.

The goal is rhythm.

Consistency beats bursts of effort every time. Ten small, steady workouts beat one heroic session. Ten steady contributions beat one random investment.

## Why Motivation Is Not the Answer

Many former athletes fall into the same trap.

They think they need more motivation.

They do not.

Motivation fades. Systems last.

During the season, you did not rely on motivation to show up to practice. You relied on structure. Training happened whether you felt like it or not. Conditioning was scheduled. Recovery was planned.

Financial discipline works the same way.

If you wait until you feel like budgeting, saving, or reviewing your finances, you are already playing from behind.

Motivation is emotional. Systems are structural.

Winning lives in structure.

## The Freedom Trap

Freedom sounds positive. But unstructured freedom often leads to pressure later.

When you control your own time without systems, small decisions accumulate. Late nights. Missed workouts. Impulse spending. Ignored paperwork. None of it feels serious.

Until it is.

Former athletes often mistake the absence of rules for the absence of consequences. In reality, consequences are simply delayed.

Structure feels restrictive in the short term. It creates freedom in the long term. Financial margin. Health. Stability. Options.

Chaos feels freeing in the short term. It creates restriction later.

## Coach's Perspective: What Would Your Coach Say?

A coach would not sugarcoat this.

"Nobody is coming to save you."

"Discipline is a choice now."

"Do your job."

"There are no off days."

"Earn everything."

The absence of structure is not freedom. It is risk.

If you do not build your own system, the default system will work against you.

## Game Situations and Decision Points

You have flexibility in your schedule. Do you use it intentionally or let it drift?

You miss a financial habit. Do you reset immediately or quit entirely?

Nobody is watching. Do you still show up?

These moments feel small. They are not.

They determine whether your financial season stays competitive or slowly falls apart.

## Common Player Mistakes and Financial Parallels

Hockey players rely on enforced accountability.

Financially, that leads to inconsistency once structure disappears.

Players underestimate how much routines matter.

Financially, that leads to drift and missed opportunities.

Players avoid building systems because they feel restrictive.

Financially, that leads to chaos disguised as freedom.

Structure is not the enemy. Lack of structure is.

## Rebuilding Structure the Right Way

Rebuilding structure does not mean recreating your old playing schedule.

It means creating systems that fit your current life.

Short, regular check-ins instead of constant monitoring

Automatic processes instead of constant decisions

Simple rules instead of complex plans

In hockey terms, this is shortening your bench but increasing efficiency. Fewer moving parts. Clear roles. Predictable execution.

The best systems are boring.

Boring systems win.

## Winning the Long Game

Rebuilding structure is one of the most important skills after hockey.

It protects your finances.

It reduces stress.

It prevents drift.

It creates freedom later.

The players who succeed after the rink closes are not the most motivated. They are the ones who replace coaches with calendars, practices with systems, and accountability with discipline.

You already know how to live inside structure.

Now you just have to build your own.

## Athlete Takeaways

When the schedule disappears, discipline becomes a choice

Optional discipline is harder than mandatory discipline

Drift breaks financial habits quietly, not all at once

Systems beat motivation every time

Build structure or let the game slip away

# Chapter 27: From Teammates to Coworkers

**One of the hardest transitions after hockey has nothing to do with skating, strength, or effort.**

**It is cultural.**

For most of your life, you lived inside a system built on clarity.

Roles were defined. Authority was obvious. Feedback was constant. Performance was visible. Ice time told the truth. If you earned it, you played. If you didn't, you sat. The scoreboard settled arguments.

Then the season ends for good.

Suddenly, you are surrounded by coworkers instead of teammates, managers instead of coaches, and meetings instead of practices. The rules feel unwritten. Feedback feels vague. Advancement feels inconsistent. And effort does not always lead directly to results.

This shift affects more than job satisfaction. It affects income growth, confidence, and long-term career stability.

## Opening Shift: A New Locker Room That Doesn't Feel Like One

Every former hockey player recognizes this moment.

You show up early. You work hard. You stay late. You assume that effort will be noticed the same way it was in the rink. You expect performance to speak for itself.

Weeks pass. Then months.

No clear feedback.

No clear role change.

No clear sense of what actually matters.

In hockey, that would never happen. Coaches communicate. Ice time reflects performance. Film exposes mistakes.

In the workplace, the feedback loop is slower, quieter, and often incomplete. If you expect the same structure you had in hockey, frustration builds fast.

It feels like skating hard with no idea where the play is going.

## Why the Workplace Feels Foreign After Sports

Hockey environments are honest.

You either win puck battles or you don't. You either backcheck or you don't. Everyone sees it. Everyone knows it.

Workplaces rarely function that way.

Performance metrics are often vague. Expectations shift without warning. Promotions are influenced by perception, timing, communication, and relationships as much as raw output. The hardest worker is not always the one who advances.

For former players, this can feel unfair or disorienting.

In hockey terms, this is playing a game with no scoreboard and no shift chart. You're skating hard, but you're not sure if it's helping or hurting your ice time.

Understanding that the game has changed is the first step to adapting.

## Authority Without Coaches

In hockey, authority is clear.

Head coach. Assistants. Captains. Everyone knows who sets the lines and makes decisions.

In many workplaces, authority is less obvious.

Titles do not always equal influence. Decision-making can be scattered. Managers may avoid confrontation. Leaders may not give direct guidance. Some people with no formal authority still control outcomes because of experience, relationships, or internal credibility.

Former players often struggle here because they wait for direction that never comes.

In hockey, waiting for instruction is normal. In the workplace, it can stall your progress. Initiative, communication, and visibility matter more.

Learning who actually makes decisions, how priorities are set, and how influence flows is essential for career growth and income stability.

## Feedback Without Film

Athletes are raised on film.

You see mistakes. You correct them. Feedback is immediate, specific, and unavoidable.

In the workplace, feedback is often delayed, softened, or avoided entirely. You may not know you are off track until a performance review, a missed promotion, or a sudden role change.

In hockey terms, this is playing an entire season without watching film and being told afterward that you were out of position all year.

Former players must adapt by asking for feedback proactively, checking assumptions, and self-evaluating honestly. Waiting for feedback to be handed to you rarely works.

Asking, "What does success look like here?" or "What would make me more valuable in this role?" becomes part of the new game.

## Politics, Ambiguity, and Unclear Expectations

Hockey has politics, but performance usually overrides them.

Workplaces are different.

Relationships matter.

Timing matters.

Perception matters.

Communication style matters.

Ignoring politics does not make them disappear. It makes you vulnerable.

Navigating workplace dynamics does not mean compromising values. It means understanding the environment so you can operate effectively within it. Smart players read the ice. Smart professionals read the room.

Understanding who influences decisions, how credit is shared, and how information flows protects your career and income.

## How This Impacts Income Growth and Career Stability

Confusion slows progress.

When expectations are unclear, you may work hard in the wrong areas. When communication is weak, your value may go unnoticed. When frustration builds, job hopping or disengagement becomes tempting.

Former hockey players who adapt tend to grow faster. They seek clarity. They build relationships. They ask questions. They advocate for themselves. They make their contributions visible.

Those who don't often feel stuck, undervalued, or burned out despite strong work ethic.

Income growth rarely comes from effort alone. It comes from aligning effort with what actually matters in the system you are in.

## Coach's Perspective

A coach would be blunt.

Learn the system.

Communicate clearly.

Ask for feedback.

Do not assume effort is visible.

Take ownership of your development.

You are still responsible for your ice time. The game just looks different now.

## Game Situations and Decision Points

You are unsure what matters most.

Do you ask for clarity or guess and hope?

You want advancement.

Do you wait quietly or communicate your goals?

You feel frustrated.

Do you disengage or adapt your approach?

Each decision compounds over time. Small adjustments in communication and awareness can change the trajectory of your career and earnings.

## Common Hockey Mistakes and Financial Parallels

Hockey players wait for direction.

Financially and professionally, that stalls income growth.

Hockey players ignore politics.

Financially, that limits opportunity and visibility.

Hockey players expect fairness.

Financially, that leads to frustration instead of strategy.

The same habits that cost ice time can cost earnings.

## Winning the Long Game

The workplace is not the locker room. The rules are different, but success is still possible.

Former hockey players who adapt without losing discipline build stable, growing careers. They learn the system, communicate effectively, and take control of their development.

You still win through preparation, awareness, and consistency.

The shift just looks different.

## Athlete Takeaways

The workplace has no scoreboard, so you must seek clarity

Authority and feedback are less obvious than in hockey

Effort alone does not guarantee advancement

Communication protects income growth

Adaptation, not frustration, builds long-term career stability

# Chapter 28: When No One Is Watching Anymore

**One of the biggest shocks after hockey is not physical.**

**It is silence.**

No crowd.

No coaches yelling from the bench.

No teammates tapping sticks on the boards.

No shift chart. No ice time. No consequences that show up immediately.

For most of your playing life, accountability was built into the environment. Miss a workout and someone noticed. Skip a rep and it showed on the ice. Take a night off mentally and you paid for it in your next shift.

Then the rink doors close for the last time.

And suddenly, no one is watching anymore.

This is where many former players struggle, not because they lost discipline, but because the system that enforced it disappeared.

## Opening Shift: Empty Rink, Full Freedom

Every former hockey player recognizes this moment.

Your schedule opens up. No mandatory lifts. No practice times. No film sessions. No coach checking attendance. You tell yourself you'll stay sharp on your own.

At first, you do.

You get to the gym. You track your meals. You keep some routines.

Then life creeps in. Work runs late. A social event pops up. You skip a workout. You put off saving. You delay planning. Nothing bad happens right away.

That delay is the trap.

In hockey terms, this is open ice with no scoreboard. You can glide if you want. You can cheat a little. You can coast. The problem is you don't notice the damage until the third period.

Freedom without structure feels good early. It gets expensive later.

## The Discipline Gap After Accountability Disappears

In hockey, accountability is constant.

Miss a backcheck and the whole bench sees it. Skip a shift change and you hear about it. Show up out of shape and the pace of practice exposes you. Structure forces discipline whether you feel motivated or not.

After sports, discipline becomes internal.

You can overspend.

You can delay investing.

You can ignore planning.

Nothing blows the whistle. No one benches you. No one reduces your minutes.

This creates a discipline gap. Not because you don't know what to do, but because no one is enforcing it anymore.

In hockey terms, this is a long season without referees or coaches. The rules still matter. They're just not enforced in real time.

## Why Former Athletes Self-Sabotage Without Pressure

Pressure sharpens focus.

Without it, comfort moves in quietly.

You start choosing ease over effort. Netflix replaces workouts. Spending replaces saving. Short-term relief replaces long-term progress. None of it feels dramatic. It feels earned.

"I worked hard for years."

"I deserve this."

"I'll tighten things up later."

Self-sabotage is rarely intentional. It shows up as drift.

Former hockey players are used to external pressure creating urgency. When that pressure disappears, many struggle to create urgency on their own.

In hockey terms, this is playing a full season of shinny. Fun at first. No intensity. No accountability. No development.

## Comfort vs Growth Decisions

Every decision sits on a spectrum between comfort and growth.

Comfort feels good now.

Growth feels uncomfortable now but pays off later.

In hockey terms, comfort is dumping the puck instead of making the hard breakout pass. Growth is staying composed under pressure and making the right play.

Financially, comfort looks like:

Spending instead of saving

Avoiding planning conversations

Ignoring long term goals

Choosing convenience over discipline

Growth looks boring in the moment. It compounds quietly.

Most money mistakes come from choosing comfort repeatedly, not from one bad decision. The cost does not show up immediately. It shows up years later, when flexibility is gone and options feel limited.

## Translating "Grind Culture" Into Adult Life

Many former players try to recreate hockey grind culture in adulthood.

They work longer hours. Push harder. Take fewer breaks. Say yes to everything. They assume effort alone will carry them.

It rarely does.

Adults are not rewarded for effort alone. They are rewarded for systems, consistency, communication, and results. Grind without structure leads to burnout, not progress.

In hockey terms, this is double-shifting every game without managing recovery. You might survive short term, but the season will catch you.

The goal is not maximum intensity.

It is sustainable discipline.

## Why Money Mistakes Show Up Years Later

Money has delayed feedback.

Overspending today creates stress years later.

Skipping saving now limits options later.

Avoiding planning compounds quietly.

In hockey terms, this is taking lazy routes early that cost you late goals. You don't feel it in the first period. You feel it when legs are heavy and the game is on the line.

This delay tricks people into thinking their habits are fine. By the time the consequences show up, they are harder to fix.

That is why discipline matters most when no one is watching.

## Building Accountability Without an Audience

The solution is not more motivation. It is structure you create yourself.

Automatic savings and investing

Scheduled financial check-ins

Clear rules for spending and debt

Defined goals with timelines

In hockey terms, this is becoming your own coach. Setting practice times. Tracking reps. Reviewing performance. No applause required.

Private discipline creates public results.

## Coach's Perspective

A coach would be honest.

Nobody is watching now.

That doesn't mean it doesn't matter.

Discipline is your responsibility.

Choose growth over comfort.

Do the work when no one is clapping.

Championship habits are built away from the spotlight.

## Game Situations and Decision Points

You're tired after work.

Do you choose comfort or discipline?

No one notices if you skip saving this month.

Do you stay consistent anyway?

The payoff feels far away.

Do you trust the process or drift?

These moments feel small. They are not.

They define outcomes more than any big decision.

## Common Hockey Mistakes and Financial Parallels

Hockey players rely on external accountability.

Financially, that leads to drift.

Hockey players chase comfort shifts.

Financially, that leads to overspending.

Hockey players confuse effort with progress.

Financially, that leads to burnout.

The habits that cost games also cost financial stability.

## Winning the Long Game

Discipline without an audience is harder, but it is more powerful.

The habits you maintain privately shape the results you see publicly. Former hockey players who rebuild structure early protect their future. They create systems that replace coaches. Calendars that replace practice plans. Rules that remove decision-making.

No one is watching.

That's the point.

## Athlete Takeaways

Accountability disappears after hockey, discipline must become internal

Comfort choices compound into long-term problems

Grind without structure leads to burnout, not progress

Money gives delayed feedback, stay disciplined anyway

What you do when no one is watching matters most

# Chapter 29: Redefining Winning After the Uniform Comes Off

**One of the biggest shocks after hockey is not physical.**

**It is silence.**

No crowd.

No coaches yelling from the bench.

No teammates tapping sticks on the boards.

No shift chart. No ice time. No consequences that show up immediately.

For most of your playing life, accountability was built into the environment. Miss a workout and someone noticed. Skip a rep and it showed on the ice. Take a night off mentally and you paid for it in your next shift.

Then the rink doors close for the last time.

And suddenly, no one is watching anymore.

This is where many former players struggle, not because they lost discipline, but because the system that enforced it disappeared.

## Opening Shift: Empty Rink, Full Freedom

Every former hockey player recognizes this moment.

Your schedule opens up. No mandatory lifts. No practice times. No film sessions. No coach checking attendance. You tell yourself you'll stay sharp on your own.

At first, you do.

You get to the gym. You track your meals. You keep some routines. You feel in control.

Then life creeps in. Work runs late. A social event pops up. You skip a workout. You put off saving. You delay planning. Nothing bad happens right away.

That delay is the trap.

In hockey terms, this is open ice with no scoreboard. You can glide if you want. You can cheat a little. You can coast. The problem is you don't notice the damage until the third period.

Freedom without structure feels good early. It gets expensive later.

## The Discipline Gap After Accountability Disappears

In hockey, accountability is constant.

Miss a backcheck and the whole bench sees it. Skip a shift change and you hear about it. Show up out of shape and the pace of practice exposes you. Structure forces discipline whether you feel motivated or not.

After sports, discipline becomes internal.

You can overspend.

You can delay investing.

You can ignore planning.

Nothing blows the whistle. No one benches you. No one reduces your minutes.

This creates a discipline gap. Not because you don't know what to do, but because no one is enforcing it anymore.

In hockey terms, this is a long season without referees or coaches. The rules still matter. They're just not enforced in real time.

## Why Former Athletes Self-Sabotage Without Pressure

Pressure sharpens focus.

Without it, comfort moves in quietly.

You start choosing ease over effort. Netflix replaces workouts. Spending replaces saving. Short-term relief replaces long-term progress. None of it feels dramatic. It feels earned.

"I worked hard for years."

"I deserve this."

"I'll tighten things up later."

Self-sabotage is rarely intentional. It shows up as drift.

Former hockey players are used to external pressure creating urgency. When that pressure disappears, many struggle to create urgency on their own.

In hockey terms, this is playing a full season of shinny. Fun at first. No intensity. No accountability. No development.

## Comfort vs Growth Decisions

Every decision sits on a spectrum between comfort and growth.

Comfort feels good now.

Growth feels uncomfortable now but pays off later.

In hockey terms, comfort is dumping the puck instead of making the hard breakout pass. Growth is staying composed under pressure and making the right play.

Financially, comfort looks like:

Spending instead of saving

Avoiding planning conversations

Ignoring long-term goals

Choosing convenience over discipline

Growth looks boring in the moment. It compounds quietly.

Most money mistakes come from choosing comfort repeatedly, not from one bad decision. The cost does not show up immediately. It shows up years later, when flexibility is gone and options feel limited.

## Translating "Grind Culture" Into Adult Life

Many former players try to recreate hockey grind culture in adulthood.

They work longer hours. Push harder. Take fewer breaks. Say yes to everything. They assume effort alone will carry them.

It rarely does.

Adults are not rewarded for effort alone. They are rewarded for systems, consistency, communication, and results. Grind without structure leads to burnout, not progress.

In hockey terms, this is double-shifting every game without managing recovery. You might survive short term, but the season will catch you.

The goal is not maximum intensity.

It is sustainable discipline.

## Why Money Mistakes Show Up Years Later

Money has delayed feedback.

Overspending today creates stress years later.

Skipping saving now limits options later.

Avoiding planning compounds quietly.

In hockey terms, this is taking lazy routes early that cost you late goals. You don't feel it in the first period. You feel it when legs are heavy and the game is on the line.

This delay tricks people into thinking their habits are fine. By the time the consequences show up, they are harder to fix.

That is why discipline matters most when no one is watching.

## Building Accountability Without an Audience

The solution is not more motivation. It is structure you create yourself.

Automatic savings and investing

Scheduled financial check-ins

Clear rules for spending and debt

Defined goals with timelines

In hockey terms, this is becoming your own coach. Setting practice times. Tracking reps. Reviewing performance. No applause required.

Private discipline creates public results.

## Coach's Perspective

A coach would be honest.

Nobody is watching now.

That doesn't mean it doesn't matter.

Discipline is your responsibility.

Choose growth over comfort.

Do the work when no one is clapping.

Championship habits are built away from the spotlight.

## Game Situations and Decision Points

You're tired after work.

Do you choose comfort or discipline?

No one notices if you skip saving this month.

Do you stay consistent anyway?

The payoff feels far away.

Do you trust the process or drift?

These moments feel small. They are not.

They define outcomes more than any big decision.

## Common Hockey Mistakes and Financial Parallels

Hockey players rely on external accountability.

Financially, that leads to drift.

Hockey players chase comfort shifts.

Financially, that leads to overspending.

Hockey players confuse effort with progress.

Financially, that leads to burnout.

The habits that cost games also cost financial stability.

## Winning the Long Game

Discipline without an audience is harder, but it is more powerful.

The habits you maintain privately shape the results you see publicly. Former hockey players who rebuild structure early protect their future. They create systems that replace coaches. Calendars that replace practice plans. Rules that remove decision-making.

No one is watching.

That's the point.

## Athlete Takeaways

Accountability disappears after hockey, discipline must become internal

Comfort choices compound into long-term problems

Grind without structure leads to burnout, not progress

Money gives delayed feedback, stay disciplined anyway

What you do when no one is watching matters most

# Chapter 30: Staying Connected Without Living in the Past

When the season ends, the rink goes quiet.

No more scheduled practices.

No more road trips.

No more locker room noise, chirping, or shared routines.

For a long time, hockey gave you built-in connection. You didn't have to search for community. It was handed to you every day you showed up to the rink. Teammates, coaches, trainers, equipment staff. A place to belong without asking for it.

When that disappears, the silence can be louder than any crowd.

## *Opening Shift: The Quiet After the Rink*

Every former player knows this moment.

You wake up on a weekday and realize no one is waiting for you. No one checks attendance. No one holds you accountable except yourself. The structure, identity, and community that once surrounded you are gone.

At first, it feels like freedom.

Then it starts to feel like isolation.

In hockey terms, this is getting sent back on the ice without linemates. You're still skating, but the game feels different. Harder. Less coordinated. Easier to drift.

This chapter is about staying connected without getting stuck.

## *Why Isolation Hits Former Athletes Hard*

Isolation does not mean being alone. It means being disconnected from people who understand you.

Hockey players are conditioned to operate in tight groups. You share pressure, pain, losses, and wins. You trust the guy next to you because he's been through the same grind.

When that environment disappears, many former players struggle to replace it. Adult life rarely offers built-in locker rooms. Workplaces can be transactional. Friendships can feel surface-level. Vulnerability is not automatic.

In hockey terms, this is playing a road game with no bench energy. You're still competing, but the support is missing.

Isolation often shows up quietly:

- Pulling back instead of reaching out
- Overworking to avoid emptiness
- Numbing with distractions, spending, or substances
- Living in memories instead of building new connections

The danger is not nostalgia. The danger is getting stuck there.

## *The Role of Community After Hockey*

Community still matters. It just has to be rebuilt intentionally.

Former players who thrive do not replace hockey with nothing. They replace it with new locker rooms. Not identical ones, but functional ones.

Community after sports might come from:

- Work teams that share purpose
- Fitness groups or rec leagues
- Mentorship circles
- Faith communities

- Business or professional groups
- Former athlete networks

In hockey terms, this is finding a new line that fits your current game. Different pace. Different roles. Same need for trust and accountability.

You don't need everyone to understand your past. You need a few people who understand your present.

## *Mentorship: From Being Coached to Being Connected*

For years, coaches guided your development. They corrected mistakes. Set expectations. Held you accountable.

After sports, many former players lose that voice.

Mentorship fills that gap.

A mentor does not replace a coach, but they provide perspective. They help you see blind spots. They remind you that growth is still possible.

Equally important is becoming a mentor yourself.

Former athletes find purpose when they pass lessons forward. Coaching youth sports. Advising younger players. Helping teammates navigate transitions.

In hockey terms, this is moving from rookie to veteran. You still compete, but you also stabilize the room.

Purpose grows when your experience matters to someone else.

## *Finding Purpose Without the Team*

One of the hardest adjustments after hockey is losing the feeling of being needed.

Teams need you. Your shift matters. Your role impacts outcomes. That sense of contribution fuels identity.

When that disappears, many former players feel replaceable.

Purpose does not disappear. It changes shape.

Purpose after sports often comes from:

- Building something long term
- Providing for others
- Solving meaningful problems
- Creating stability
- Teaching and leading

In hockey terms, this is shifting from chasing goals to protecting the lead. Different role. Same importance.

Purpose is not about adrenaline. It's about responsibility.

### *Healthy Nostalgia vs Being Stuck*

Missing hockey is normal.

Talking about old games. Laughing about road trips. Remembering teammates. That's healthy nostalgia. It honors what shaped you.

Being stuck looks different.

Being stuck sounds like:

- "Those were the best years of my life."
- "Nothing compares to that."
- "I peaked back then."

In hockey terms, this is replaying old highlights instead of watching current game film. It feels good, but it doesn't help you win today.

Healthy nostalgia coexists with forward motion. Being stuck replaces forward motion.

You don't need to forget hockey. You need to stop living there.

### *Creating a Forward-Looking Identity*

Your hockey identity was clear. Position. Role. Expectations.

After sports, identity becomes self-defined. That freedom is powerful and uncomfortable.

Former players struggle when they cling to who they were instead of building who they are becoming.

A forward-looking identity answers new questions:

- What do I value now?
- What kind of life am I building?
- What does success look like in this season?

In hockey terms, this is adjusting your game as your role changes. You don't play the same way at every stage of your career. You adapt.

Your discipline. Work ethic. Mental toughness. Those still belong to you. The uniform does not.

## *Coach's Perspective*

A coach would be blunt.

Stop waiting for the team to come back.

Build the next one.

Use what hockey gave you.

Don't let it trap you.

You're not done competing. You're just competing differently now.

## *Game Situations and Decision Points*

You feel disconnected at work.

Do you isolate or build relationships?

You miss the locker room.

Do you live in memories or create new routines?

You see younger players coming up.

Do you envy them or mentor them?

Every choice either moves you forward or keeps you stuck.

## *Common Hockey Mistakes and Life Parallels*

Players cling to old roles too long.

Former athletes cling to old identities.

Players blame coaches instead of adapting.

Adults blame circumstances instead of building community.

Players lose purpose without ice time.

Adults lose direction without structure.

The pattern repeats unless you interrupt it.

## *Winning the Long Game*

Staying connected is not about recreating the past. It is about carrying the best parts of it forward.

Hockey taught you how to belong, commit, and contribute. Those skills still matter. They just need new environments.

The players who thrive after the rink are not the ones who forget hockey. They are the ones who refuse to let it define their ceiling.

The game gave you tools.

Now you decide how to use them.

## *Athlete Takeaways*

- Isolation fades when you intentionally build new locker rooms
- Mentorship gives direction when coaching disappears
- Nostalgia is healthy unless it replaces forward motion
- Purpose comes from contribution, not adrenaline
- Your identity evolves, but your discipline stays with you

# Glossary of Hockey and Financial Terms

This glossary connects key financial concepts to familiar ideas from **hockey**, making money easier to understand through the language, structure, and discipline players already know.

## *Asset Allocation*

**Financial Definition:**

How money is divided among different investment types such as stocks, bonds, and cash to balance risk and return.

**Hockey Comparison:**

Line combinations and ice time distribution. Too much reliance on one line or one player throws the whole game out of balance.

## *Assets*

**Financial Definition:**

Things you own that have value, such as cash, investments, real estate, or retirement accounts.

**Hockey Comparison:**

Your tools as a player. Skating ability, conditioning, hockey IQ, experience, and preparation that contribute to overall performance.

### *Bonds*

**Financial Definition:**

Loans made to governments or companies that pay interest and return principal over time.

**Hockey Comparison:**

Responsible defensive play. Not flashy, but essential for protecting the lead and stabilizing the game.

### *Budget*

**Financial Definition:**

A plan for how income is allocated toward expenses, savings, and goals.

**Hockey Comparison:**

Shift management. If you don't manage time and energy, you're gassed when it matters most.

### *Cash Flow*

**Financial Definition:**

Money coming in versus money going out.

**Hockey Comparison:**

Stamina over a game and season. Burn too much energy early and you struggle to finish strong.

### *Compounding*

**Financial Definition:**

Earnings that generate additional earnings over time.

**Hockey Comparison:**

Daily reps. Small improvements stacked over time turn average players into reliable contributors.

### *Credit*

**Financial Definition:**

The ability to borrow money with the promise of repayment.

**Hockey Comparison:**

Trust from the coach. Earned through consistency and discipline, lost quickly when abused.

### *Debt*

**Financial Definition:**

Money borrowed that must be repaid, often with interest.

**Hockey Comparison:**

Playing hurt. Sometimes manageable short term, but dangerous if it lingers or gets ignored.

### *Diversification*

**Financial Definition:**

Spreading investments across different assets to reduce risk.

**Hockey Comparison:**

Rolling four lines instead of overplaying one. Depth keeps you competitive through a long season.

### *Emergency Fund*

**Financial Definition:**

Savings set aside for unexpected expenses.

**Hockey Comparison:**

A reliable backup goalie. You hope you never need them, but you're grateful when you do.

### *ETF (Exchange-Traded Fund)*

**Financial Definition:**

A fund that holds many investments and trades like a stock.

**Hockey Comparison:**

A full line working together instead of a solo rush up the ice.

### *Fees / Expense Ratios*

**Financial Definition:**

Costs associated with managing investments.

**Hockey Comparison:**

Sloppy line changes. Small mistakes that quietly give up momentum and goals over time.

### *Growth Investing*

**Financial Definition:**

Investing in companies expected to grow faster than average.

**Hockey Comparison:**

Playing an aggressive offensive style. Higher upside, but it requires discipline and strong fundamentals.

### *Insurance*

**Financial Definition:**

Protection against financial loss from unexpected events.

**Hockey Comparison:**

Protective equipment. You don't skip it just because nothing has gone wrong yet.

*Liquidity*

**Financial Definition:**

How easily money can be accessed without penalty or delay.

**Hockey Comparison:**

Quick line changes. Flexibility to respond when the pace of the game shifts.

*Net Worth*

**Financial Definition:**

Assets minus liabilities.

**Hockey Comparison:**

The scoreboard at the end of the game. Not one shift, but the total result.

*Rebalancing*

**Financial Definition:**

Adjusting investments back to their intended mix over time.

**Hockey Comparison:**

Mid-season lineup adjustments to restore balance and consistency.

*Risk*

**Financial Definition:**

The chance that outcomes differ from expectations, including loss.

**Hockey Comparison:**

Shot selection. The harder the shot, the more upside, but also more risk if it misses.

*Roth IRA*

**Financial Definition:**

A retirement account where money grows tax-free if rules are followed.

**Hockey Comparison:**

Extra work in training camp so the season feels easier later.

*Stocks*

**Financial Definition:**

Ownership shares in a company.

**Hockey Comparison:**

Top-line forwards. They drive scoring but still need defense and support to win games.

*Tax-Advantaged Accounts*

**Financial Definition:**

Accounts that provide tax benefits, often with rules and restrictions.

**Hockey Comparison:**

Structured systems. The rules exist to improve outcomes if you follow them.

*Volatility*

**Financial Definition:**

Short-term ups and downs in market value.

**Hockey Comparison:**

Momentum swings. Normal in every game unless you panic and abandon the plan.

### *Permanent Loss*

**Financial Definition:**
Money that cannot recover due to poor decisions or panic.
**Hockey Comparison:**
A blown assignment leading to a goal against. Usually caused by ignoring fundamentals.

### *Total Return*

**Financial Definition:**
Investment return from both price growth and income.
**Hockey Comparison:**
Winning the game, not just scoring goals. Every part of the performance matters.

### *Value Investing*

**Financial Definition:**
Investing in assets believed to be undervalued.
**Hockey Comparison:**
Reliable two-way players. Less flash, more consistency, long-term impact.

### *Yield*

**Financial Definition:**
Income generated from an investment.
**Hockey Comparison:**
Steady goal production. Not always highlight-worthy, but dependable.

## *Final Note*

This glossary reinforces one core principle:

Financial success, like success in **hockey**, comes from balance, discipline, timing, and repetition.

That philosophy runs through **Hockey Money 101** and carries forward long after the final buzzer.

# Disclaimers

## *Educational Purpose Only*

This book is for **educational purposes only**.

The information provided in **Hockey Money 101** is intended to help readers understand general financial concepts using hockey-based analogies. It is **not** individualized financial, investment, tax, legal, or insurance advice.

Every financial situation is different. Your goals, income, family circumstances, risk tolerance, career length, and time horizon are unique. What works for one player, family, or professional may not be appropriate for another.

## *Not Financial, Investment, or Legal Advice*

Nothing in this book should be interpreted as a recommendation to buy, sell, or hold any specific investment, financial product, insurance policy, or strategy.

This book does **not** replace advice from qualified professionals, including but not limited to:

- Financial advisors
- Accountants or tax professionals
- Attorneys
- Insurance professionals

Before making financial decisions, readers should consult professionals who can evaluate their individual situation and provide advice tailored to their needs.

## *No Guarantees or Promises of Results*

All investing involves risk, including the possible loss of principal.

Past performance does not guarantee future results. Markets fluctuate. Economic conditions change. Injuries, career transitions, and life events happen. Outcomes cannot be predicted or guaranteed.

The examples, comparisons, and scenarios in this book are **illustrative only** and may not reflect actual results or real-world outcomes. They are included to explain concepts, not to promise results.

## *Tax and Legal Information*

Any discussion of taxes, retirement accounts, estate planning, business structures, or legal topics is **general in nature**.

Tax laws and regulations change frequently and vary by jurisdiction. Legal requirements differ based on location, employment status, income sources, and personal circumstances.

Readers should seek personalized tax or legal advice before acting on any information related to these topics.

## *Athlete and Career Considerations*

This book discusses financial topics as they relate to athletes and former athletes, including career transitions, contract income, and post-playing life.

It does **not** provide:

- Career placement services
- Employment guarantees
- Contract negotiation services
- Promises related to income, compensation, endorsements, or career

success

Athletic careers vary widely in length, stability, and earnings. Financial planning should account for uncertainty, not assume ideal outcomes.

### *Use of Analogies*

Hockey and sports analogies are used to make financial concepts easier to understand.

These analogies are **educational tools only** and should not be interpreted literally. Financial decisions require analysis beyond analogy, including math, rules, risk assessment, and professional judgment.

The purpose of analogy is clarity, not simplification of responsibility.

### *Personal Responsibility*

By reading this book, you acknowledge that:

- You are responsible for your own financial decisions
- You understand that financial outcomes involve uncertainty and risk
- You agree to seek appropriate professional guidance when needed

Education improves decision-making, but responsibility remains with the individual.

No book, coach, or advisor can take a shift for you.

### *Contact Information*

If you would like to learn more about the concepts discussed in this book or explore additional educational resources, Pat Brown can be found through public platforms including LinkedIn, Twitter, and via Google search.

For questions specifically related to **Hockey Money 101**, you may contact: **info@hockeymoney101.com**

## *Final Reminder*

Financial success is built the same way hockey careers are built:

Through discipline, preparation, consistency, and smart adjustments over time.

This book provides a **framework**, not a guarantee.

Use it as a guide, not a substitute for professional advice.

Winning with money, like winning on the ice, comes from playing the long game one shift at a time.

*Pat Brown OLB, University of Kansas*

Made in the USA
Monee, IL
04 November 2026

67387606R00115